FIRST THROUGH
THE GRAND
CANYON

By MAJOR JOHN WESLEY POWELL

1915

Contents

PUBLISHER'S NOTES

John Wesley Powell (March 24, 1834–September 23, 1902) is one of those rare 19th-century figures whose fame has endured for almost 120 years after his death. Many of his contemporaries who were widely known during his lifetime are now entirely unknown to Americans.

The adventure you're about to read is in good measure responsible for Powell's stature in American science and exploration. Despite his loss of an arm at the Battle of Shiloh in the Civil War, it seemed nothing could slow Powell down. His wounds caused him discomfort for the rest of his life but, as you'll read, that did not stop him from clambering up cliffs and canyons.

This narrative is nearly as exhausting to read as it is exciting. The men of the Grand Canyon expedition endured incredible challenges along a very dangerous route from Wyoming to the end of their trip. By the end, they had lost three members who had had enough and the remaining crews were nearly out of food.

It's easy for the millions of annual visitors to Grand Canyon National Park to underestimate the raw danger of the 1869 expedition. Today there are guided raft trips along the canyon that can make it all seem like a joy ride. There was no assurance for Powell and his men that they would survive. No one of their time knew the canyon, there were no maps, and even Native Americans told them the canyon could not be navigated.

Yet they persisted and made history. Powell went on another expedition the next year, notes of which are included at the end of this volume. He spent the rest of his life exploring, teaching, and advocating for the preservation and conservation of public lands. From 1881–1894 he was the Director of the United States Geological Survey.

The United States Geological Survey has a superb map and legend of the entire journey at https://eros.usgs.gov/image-gallery/story-maps/150th-anniversary-jw-powells-perilous-river-expedition.

INTRODUCTION

The editor of this work, Horace Sowers Kephart (1862–1931) was a travel writer, outdoor adventurer, and advocate for the establishment of the Great Smoky Mountains National Park.

The Colorado River of the West is formed in southeastern Utah by the junction of the Grand and Green rivers. For hundreds of miles it flows through a series of profound chasms, in many places from 4,000 to 6,000 feet deep, and rising nearly vertically for a considerable distance above the water. These cañons are from one to fifteen miles wide at the top. The most famous of them is the Marble-Grand cañon (really continuous, although it goes under two names, the Marble and the Grand). Through this vast gorge the Colorado drops 2,330 feet in 283 miles, the current sometimes attaining a velocity of twenty-five miles an hour. The river itself varies in width from seventy-five feet to a quarter of a mile. In the narrowest places it has at times a depth of over 100 feet.

Up to 1869 practically nothing was known of the Colorado River from its source to where it emerges into the valley of the Grand Wash, except what could be observed from look-out points at the tops of the cañons, or from the few places where descents had been made to the bottom. It was a river of mystery and of fear. For long distances it was supposed to flow underground. There was no evidence that any human being had ever passed through the cañons and come out alive. The Indians who lived in the neighborhood considered such a feat preposterous.

Then came a scientist and a man of nerve, Major John Wesley Powell, who studied the river carefully at several points along its bank, and calmly decided to risk his life in clearing up the mystery by navigating the stream clear through to the Wash.

The undertaking was all the more remarkable from the fact that Powell had only one arm. He had lost his right arm in the battle of Shiloh. His plucky young wife,[1] to whom he had been married but a

---

[1] Emma Dean (1836–1924) with whom Powell had one daughter, Mary (born Salt Lake City, UT, never married, 1871–1959). All three Powells are buried together at Arlington National Cemetery.

2

month, was present at headquarters when he was wounded, and promptly offered herself as a substitute for the missing limb so that her husband could continue in service. She then and there enlisted, and General Grant gave her a "perpetual pass" to follow the army in the capacity she had chosen. With this help Major Powell continued in active service to the close of the war.

In his student days Powell had made a specialty of what was then called "natural history." When the war was over he accepted a professorship of geology in the Illinois Wesleyan University, and later held a similar chair in the Illinois Normal University. In the summer of 1867 he initiated the practice of student field work by taking his class to the mountains of Colorado for geological exploration. It was on this trip that he formed the idea of exploring the cañons of the Colorado River of the West.

Having obtained funds from public institutions of Illinois to outfit his little expedition, he started from Green River City, above the head of the Colorado proper, May 24, 1869, on one of the most hazardous adventures in the history of exploration. He emerged from the Grand cañon on August 29, with five of the nine men he had started with. Four had deserted on the way, and three of these were killed by Indians.

Major Powell's report on this first exploration of the Colorado River was published by the Smithsonian Institution in 1875. Together with the scientific data appended, it forms a large quarto volume, which is now out of print. The narrative part is here republished without abridgement.

In 1870, Congress established a Topographical and Geological Survey of the Colorado River of the West, and Powell was placed in charge of it. In 1871-1872 he made a second descent of the river, this time for the government. Again he came through unharmed, proving his mastery of a species of navigation so difficult that many who have tried it in later years have perished in those brawling waters.

Much of Powell's attention was given to American ethnology, and when a Bureau of Ethnology was formed by the government, he was appointed its director. In 1881 he succeeded Clarence King as director of the U. S. Geological Survey. Major Powell died September 23, 1902..

THE VALLEY OF THE COLORADO

THE Colorado River is formed by the junction of the Grand and Green.

The Grand River has its source in the Rocky Mountains, five or six miles west of Long's Peak, in latitude 40° 17' and longitude 105° 4y approximately. A group of little alpine lakes, that receive their waters directly from perpetual snow-banks, discharge into a common reservoir, known as Grand Lake, a beautiful sheet of water. Its quiet surface reflects towering cliffs and crags of granite on its eastern shore; and stately pines and firs stand on its western margin.

The Green River heads near Fremont's Peak, in the Wind River Mountains, in latitude 43° 15' and longitude 109° 45', approximately. This river, like the last, has its sources in alpine lakes, fed by everlasting snows. Thousands of these little lakes, with deep, cold, emerald waters, are embosomed among the crags of the Rocky Mountains. These streams, born in the cold, gloomy solitudes of the upper mountain region, have a strange, eventful history as they pass down through gorges, tumbling in cascades and cataracts, until they reach the hot, arid plains of the Lower Colorado, where the waters that were so clear above empty as turbid floods into the Gulf of California.

The mouth of the Colorado is in latitude 31° 53' and longitude 115°.

The Green River is larger than the Grand, and is the upper continuation of the Colorado. Including this river, the whole length of the stream is about two thousand miles. The region of country drained by the Colorado and its tributaries is about eight hundred miles in length, and varies from three hundred to five hundred in width, containing about three hundred thousand square miles, an area larger than all the New England and Middle States, and Maryland and Virginia added, or as large as Minnesota, Wisconsin, Iowa, Illinois, and Missouri.

There are two distinct portions of the basin of the Colorado. The lower third is but little above the level of the sea, though here and there ranges of mountains rise to an altitude of from two to six thousand feet. This part of the valley is bounded on the north by a line of cliffs that present a bold, often vertical step, hundreds or thousands of feet to the table-lands above.

The upper two-thirds of the basin rises from four to eight thousand feet above the level of the sea. This high region, on the east, north, and west, is set with ranges of snow-clad mountains, attaining an altitude above the sea varying from eight to fourteen thousand feet. All winter long, on its mountain-crested rim, snow falls, filling the gorges, half burying the forests, and covering the crags and peaks with a mantle woven by the winds from the waves of the sea—a mantle of snow. When the summer-sun comes, this snow melts, and tumbles down the mountain-sides in millions of cascades. Ten million cascade brooks unite to form ten thousand torrent creeks; ten thousand torrent creeks unite to form a hundred rivers beset with cataracts; a hundred roaring rivers unite to form the Colorado, which rolls, a mad, turbid stream, into the Gulf of California.

Consider the action of one of these streams: its source in the mountains, where the snows fall; its course through the arid plains. Now, if at the river's flood storms were falling on the plains, its channel would be cut but little faster than the adjacent country would be washed, and the general level would thus be preserved; but, under the conditions here mentioned, the river deepens its bed, as there is much through corrosion and but little lateral degradation.

So all the streams cut deeper and still deeper until their banks are towering cliffs of solid rock. These deep, narrow gorges are called cañons.

For more than a thousand miles along its course, the Colorado has cut for itself such a cañon; but at some few points, where lateral streams join it, the cañon is broken, and narrow, transverse valleys divide it properly into a series of cañons.

The Virgin, Kanab, Paria, Escalante, Dirty Devil, San Rafael, Price, and Uinta on the west, the Grand, Yampa, San Juan, and Colorado Chiquito on the east, have also cut for themselves such narrow, winding gorges, or deep cañons. Every river entering these has cut another cañon; every lateral creek has cut a cañon; every brook runs in a cañon; every rill born of a shower, and born again of a shower, and living only during these showers, has cut for itself a cañon; so that the whole upper portion of the basin of the Colorado is traversed by a labyrinth of these deep gorges.

Owing to a great variety of geological conditions, these cañons differ much in general aspect. The Rio Virgin, between Long Valley and the Mormon town of Schunesburgh, runs through Pa-ru'-nu-weap cañon, often not more than twenty or thirty feet in width, and from six hundred to one thousand five hundred feet deep.

Away to the north, the Yampa empties into the Green by a cañon that I essayed to cross in the fall of 1868, and was baffled from day to day until the fourth had nearly passed before I could find my way down to the river. But thirty miles above its mouth, this cañon ends, and a narrow valley, with a flood-plain, is found. Still farther up the stream, the river comes down through another cañon, and beyond that a narrow valley is found, and its upper course is now through a cañon and now a valley.

All these cañons are alike changeable in their topographic characteristics.

The longest cañon through which the Colorado runs is that between the mouth of the Colorado Chiquito and the Grand Wash, a distance of two hundred and seventeen and a half miles. But this is separated from another above, sixty-five and a half miles in length, only by the narrow cañon-valley of the Colorado Chiquito.

All the scenic features of this cañon land are on a giant scale, strange and weird. The streams run at depths almost inaccessible; lashing the rocks which beset their channels; rolling in rapids, and plunging in falls, and making a wild music which but adds to the gloom of the solitude.

The little valleys nesting along the streams are diversified by bordering willows, clumps of box-elder, and small groves of cottonwood.

Low mesas, dry and treeless, stretch back from the brink of the cañon, often showing smooth surfaces of naked, solid rock. In some places, the country rock being composed of marls, the surface is a bed of loose, disintegrated material, and you walk through it as in a bed of ashes. Often these marls are richly colored and variegated. In other places, the country rock is a loose sandstone, the disintegration of which has left broad stretches of drifting sand, white, golden, and vermilion.

Where this sandstone is a conglomerate, a paving of pebbles has been left, a mosaic of many colors, polished by the drifting sands, and glistening in the sunlight.

After the cañons, the most remarkable features of the country are the long lines of cliffs. These are bold escarpments, often hundreds or thousands of feet in altitude, great geographic steps, scores or hundreds of miles in length, presenting steep faces of rock, often quite vertical.

Having climbed one of these steps, you may descend by a gentle, sometimes imperceptible, slope to the foot of another. They will thus present a series of terraces, the steps of which are well-defined escarpments of rock. The lateral extension of such a line of cliffs is usually very irregular; sharp salients are projected on the plains below, and deep recesses are cut into the terraces above.

Intermittent streams coming down the cliffs have cut many cañons or cañon valleys, by which the traveler may pass from the plain below to the terrace above. By these gigantic stairways, you may ascend to high plateaus, covered with forests of pine and fir.

The region is further diversified by short ranges of eruptive mountains. A vast system of fissures—huge cracks in the rocks to the depths below—extends across the country. From these crevices, floods of lava have poured, covering mesas and table-lands with sheets of black basalt. The expiring energies of these volcanic agencies have piled up huge cinder-cones, that stand along the fissures, red, brown, and black, naked of vegetation, and conspicuous landmarks, set, as they are, in contrast to the bright, variegated rocks of sedimentary origin.

These cañon gorges, obstructing cliffs and desert wastes, have prevented the traveler from penetrating the country, so that, until the Colorado River Exploring Expedition was organized, it was almost unknown. Yet enough had been seen to foment rumor, and many wonderful stories have been told in the hunter's cabin and prospector's camp. Stories were related of parties entering the gorge in boats, and being carried down with fearful velocity into whirlpools, where all were overwhelmed in the abyss of waters; others, of underground passages for the great river, into which boats had passed never to be seen again. It was currently believed that the river was lost under the rocks for several hundred miles. There were other accounts of great falls, whose roaring music could be heard on the distant mountain-summits. There were many stories current of parties wandering on the brink of the cañon, vainly endeavoring to reach the waters below, and perishing with thirst at last in sight of the river which was roaring its mockery into dying ears.

The Indians, too, have woven the mysteries of the cañons into the myths of their religion. Long ago, there was a great and wise chief, who mourned the death of his wife, and would not be comforted until Ta-vwoats, one of the Indian gods, came to him, and told him she was in a happier land, and offered to take him there, that he might see for himself, if, upon his return, he would cease to mourn. The great chief promised. Then Ta-vwoats made a trail through the mountains that intervene between that beautiful land and this, the desert home of the poor Nu'-ma.

This trail was the cañon gorge of the Colorado. Through it he led him; and, when they had returned, the deity exacted from the chief a promise that he would tell no one of the joys of that land, lest, through discontent with the circumstances of this world, they should desire to go to heaven. Then he rolled a river into the gorge, a mad, raging stream, that should engulf any that might attempt to enter thereby.

More than once have I been warned by the Indians not to enter this cañon. They considered it disobedience to the gods and contempt for their authority, and believed that it would surely bring upon me their wrath.

For two years previous to the exploration, I had been making some geological studies among the heads of the cañons leading to the Colorado, and a desire to explore the Grand cañon itself grew upon me. Early in the spring of 1869, a small party was organized for this purpose. Boats were built in Chicago, and transported by rail to the point where the Union Pacific Railroad crosses the Green River.[1] With these we were to descend the Green into the Colorado, and the Colorado down to the foot of the Grand cañon.

---

[1] Which is still does in the 21st century at the town of Green River, WY.

FROM GREEN RIVER CITY TO FLAMING GORGE

MAY 24, 1869.—The good people of Green River City turn out to see us start.[1] We raise our little flag, push the boats from shore, and the swift current carries us down.

Our boats are four in number. Three are built of oak; stanch and firm; double-ribbed, with double stem and stern posts, and further strengthened by bulkheads, dividing each into three compartments.

Two of these, the fore and aft, are decked, forming water-tight cabins. It is expected these will buoy the boats should the waves roll over them in rough water. The little vessels are twenty-one feet long, and, taking out the cargoes, can be carried by four men.

The fourth boat is made of pine, very light, but sixteen feet in length, with a sharp cut-water,[2] and every way built for fast rowing, and divided into compartments as the others.

We take with us rations deemed sufficient to last ten months; for we expect, when winter comes on and the river is filled with ice, to lie over at some point until spring arrives; so we take with us abundant supplies of clothing. We have also a large quantity of ammunition and two or three dozen traps. For the purpose of building cabins, repairing boats, and meeting other exigencies, we are supplied with axes, hammers, saws, augers, and other tools, and a quantity of nails and screws. For scientific work, we have two sextants, four chronometers, a number of barometers, thermometers, compasses, and other instruments.

The flour is divided into three equal parts; the meat and all other articles of our rations in the same way. Each of the larger boats has an ax, hammer, saw, auger, and other tools, so that all are loaded alike. We distribute the cargoes in this way, that we may not be entirely destitute of some important article should any one of the boats be lost. In the small boat, we pack a part of the scientific instruments, three guns, and three small bundles of clothing only. In this, I proceed in advance, to explore the channel.

---

[1] See cover image of the start at Green River. Powell was 35 years old.
[2] The forward curve of the stem of a ship or boat.

J. C. Sumner[3] and William H. Dunn[4] are my boatmen in the *Emma Dean*; then follows *Kitty Clyde's[5] Sister*, manned by W. H. Powell[6] and G. Y. Bradley;[7] next, the *No Name*, with O. G. Howland, Seneca Howland,[8] and Frank Goodman;[9] and last comes the *Maid of the Cañon*, with W. R. Hawkins[10] and Andrew Hall.[11]

Our boats are heavily loaded, and only with the utmost care is it possible to float in the rough river without shipping water.

A mile or two below town, we run on a sand-bar. The men jump into the stream, and thus lighten the vessels, so that they drift over;

---

[3] John Colton "Jack" Sumner (1840–1907), a hunter, trader, and Civil War veteran of the 32nd Iowa Infantry. He was apparently greatly disturbed for the rest of his life by the loss of three men on the expedition (Ross, 2018).

[4] Colorado mountain man, William H. "Bill" Dunn (1845–1869) was a Civil War veteran who left the expedition and was killed with the Howland brothers, whether by Indians or Mormons is in dispute and will never be known.

[5] Kitty Clyde was a fictional figure from a popular song of the day.

[6] Walter Powell (1841–1915), John Wesley's younger brother, a school teacher. He was also a Civil War veteran.

[7] George Young Bradley (1836–1885) had been a shoemaker before the Civil War, in which he served the Union. He served after the war until agreeing to accompany Powell if he could get a discharge from the army. He met Powell while serving in Wyoming and kept a secret diary of the trip. His diary states he once used his drawers as a rope to help the one-armed Powell up a canyon wall.

[8] The brothers, printer Oramel G. Howland (1833–1869) and Civil War veteran Seneca Howland (1843–1869) left the expedition in August and were reported killed by Indians in September.

[9] Goodman is an elusive figure and left the expedition three weeks after starting.

[10] William "Billy" Robert Wesley Hawkins (1845–1919) had been a recruit in the 15th Missouri Cavalry in the Civil War. He was described by contemporaries as "impish and indefatigable." Some historians have described him as the most colorful figure on the expedition. He was the expedition cook. He later converted to Mormonism and was the father of eleven children.

[11] Scotsman Andrew Hall (1848–1882) was the youngest member of the team. He was described by the other men as brave and full of fun. He was later in law enforcement and worked as a Wells Fargo messenger. In the latter job, he was killed by outlaw Cicero Grimes during a robbery. There is a biographical marker in the Globe, AZ cemetery noting he is buried in an unmarked grave there. Actor Richard Boone played an outlaw named Cicero Grimes in the superb 1967 Paul Newman western film *Hombre*.

and on we go. In trying to avoid a rock, an oar is broken on one of the boats, and, thus crippled, she strikes. The current is swift, and she is sent reeling and rocking into the eddy. In the confusion, two others are lost overboard and the men seem quite discomfited, much to the amusement of the other members of the party.

Catching the oars and starting again, the boats are once more borne down the stream until we land at a small cottonwood grove on the bank and camp for noon.

During the afternoon, we run down to a point where the river sweeps the foot of an overhanging cliff, and here we camp for the night. The sun is yet two hours high, so I climb the cliffs, and walk back among the strangely carved rocks of the Green River badlands. These are sandstones and shales, gray and buff, red and brown, blue and black strata in many alternations, lying nearly horizontal, and almost without soil and vegetation. They are very friable, and the rain and streams have carved them into quaint shapes. Barren desolation is stretched before me; and yet there is a beauty in the scene. The fantastic carving, imitating architectural forms, and suggesting rude but weird statuary, with the bright and varied colors of the rocks, conspire to make a scene such as the dweller in verdure-clad hills can scarcely appreciate.

Standing on a high point, I can look off in every direction over a vast landscape, with salient rocks and cliffs glittering in the evening sun. Dark shadows are settling in the valleys and gulches, and the heights are made higher and the depths deeper by the glamour and witchery of light and shade.

Away to the south, the Uinta Mountains stretch in a long line; high peaks thrust into the sky, and snow-fields glittering like lakes of molten silver; and pine-forests in somber green; and rosy clouds playing around the borders of huge, black masses; and heights and clouds, and mountains and snow-fields, and forests and rock-lands, are blended into one grand view. Now the sun goes down, and I return to camp.

May 25.—We start early this morning, and run along at a good rate until about nine o'clock, when we are brought up on a gravelly bar.

All jump out, and help the boats over by main strength. Then a rain comes on, and river and clouds conspire to give us a thorough drenching. Wet, chilled, and tired to exhaustion, we stop at a cottonwood grove on the bank, build a huge fire, make a cup of coffee, and are soon refreshed and quite merry. When the clouds "get out of our sunshine," we start again. A few miles farther down, a flock of mountain-sheep are seen on a cliff to the right. The boats are quietly tied up, and three or four men go after them. In the course of two or three hours, they return. The cook has been successful in bringing down a fat lamb. The unsuccessful hunters taunt him with finding it dead; but it is soon dressed, cooked, and eaten, making a fine four o'clock dinner.

"All aboard," and down the river for another dozen miles. On the way, we pass the mouth of Black's Fork,[12] a dirty little stream that seems somewhat swollen. Just below its mouth, we land and camp.

May 26.—today, we pass several curiously-shaped buttes, standing between the west bank of the river and the high bluffs beyond. These buttes are outliers of the same beds of rocks exposed on the faces of the bluffs; thinly laminated shales and sandstones of many colors, standing above in vertical cliffs, and buttressed below with a water-carved talus; some of them attain an altitude of nearly a thousand feet above the level of the river.

We glide quietly down the placid stream past the carved cliffs of the *mauvaises terres*, now and then obtaining glimpses of distant mountains. Occasionally, deer are started from the glades among the willows; and several wild geese, after a chase through the water, are shot.

After dinner, we pass through a short, narrow cañon into a broad valley; from this, long, lateral valleys stretch back on either side as far as the eye can reach.

Two or three miles below, Henry's Fork enters from the right. We land a short distance above the junction, where a *cache* of instruments and rations was made several months ago, in a cave at

---

12 In the 21st century, this is under the Flaming Gorge Reservoir.

the foot of the cliff, a distance back from the river. Here it was safe from the elements and wild beasts, but not from man. Some anxiety is felt, as we have learned that a party of Indians have been camped near it for several weeks. Our fears are soon allayed, for we find it all right. Our chronometer wheels are not taken for hair ornaments; our barometer tubes, for beads; nor the sextant thrown into the river as "bad medicine," as had been predicted.

Taking up our *cache* we pass down to the foot of the Uinta Mountains, and, in a cold storm, go into camp.

The river is running to the south;[13] the mountains have an easterly and westerly trend directly athwart its course, yet it glides on in a quiet way as if it thought a mountain range no formidable obstruction to its course. It enters the range by a flaring, brilliant, red gorge, that may be seen from the north a score of miles away.

The great mass of the mountain-ridge through which the gorge is cut is composed of bright vermilion rocks; but they are surmounted by broad bands of mottled buff and gray, and these bands come down with a gentle curve to the water's edge on the nearer slope of the mountain.

This is the head of the first cañon we are about to explore—an introductory one to a series made by the river through this range. We name it Flaming Gorge. The cliffs or walls we find, on measurement, to be about one thousand two hundred feet high.

May 27.—Today it rains, and we employ the time in repairing one of our barometers, which was broken on the way from New York. A new tube has to be put in; that is, a long glass tube has to be filled with mercury four or five inches at a time, and each installment boiled over a spirit-lamp. It is a delicate task to do this without breaking the glass; but we have success, and are ready to measure the mountains once more.

May 28.—Today we go to the summit of the cliff on the left and take observations for altitude, and are variously employed in topographic and geological work.

---

[13] The river turns to the south here just below Taylor Flats in Utah.

May 29—This morning, Bradley and I cross the river, and climb more than a thousand feet to a point where we can see the stream sweeping in a long, beautiful curve through the gorge below. Turning and looking to the west, we can see the valley of Henry's Fork, through which, for many miles, the little river flows in a tortuous channel. Cottonwood groves are planted here and there along its course, and between them are stretches of grass land. The narrow mountain valley is inclosed on either side by sloping walls of naked rock of many bright colors. To the south of the valley are the Uintas, and the peaks of the Wasatch Mountains can be faintly seen in the far west. To the north, desert plains, dotted here and there with curiously carved hills and buttes, extend to the limit of vision.

For many years, this valley has been the home of a number of mountaineers, who were originally hunters and trappers, living with the Indians. Most of them have one or more Indian wives. They no longer roam with the nomadic tribes in pursuit of buckskin or beaver, but have accumulated herds of cattle and horses, and consider themselves quite well-to-do. Some of them have built cabins; others still live in lodges.

John Baker[14] is one of the most famous of these men; and, from our point of view, we can see his lodge three or four miles up the river.

The distance from Green River City to Flaming Gorge is sixty-two miles. The river runs between bluffs, in some places standing so close to each other that no flood-plain is seen. At such a point, the river might properly be said to run through a cañon. The bad-lands on either side are interrupted here and there by patches of *Artemesia*, or sage-brush. Where there is a flood-plain along either side of the river, a few cottonwoods may be seen.

---

[14] Powell may be referring to the brother of famous frontiersman Jim Baker (1818–1898).

FROM FLAMING GORGE TO THE GATE OF LODORE

YOU must not think of a mountain-range as a line of peaks standing on a plain, but as a broad platform many miles wide, from which mountains have been carved by the waters. You must conceive, too, that this plateau is cut by gulches and cañons in many directions, and that beautiful valleys are scattered about at different altitudes. The first series of cañons we are about to explore constitutes a river channel through such a range of mountains. The cañon is cut nearly half-way through the range, then turns to the east, and is cut along the central line, or axis, gradually crossing it to the south. Keeping this direction for more than fifty miles,[1] it then turns abruptly to a southwest course, and goes diagonally through the southern slope of the range.

This much we knew before entering, as we made a partial exploration of the region last fall, climbing many of its peaks, and in a few places reaching the brink of the cañon walls, and looking over the precipices, many hundreds of feet high, to the water below.

Here and there the walls are broken by lateral cañons, the channels of little streams entering the river; through two or three of these, we found our way down to the Green in early winter, and walked along the low, water-beach at the foot of the cliffs for several miles. Where the river has this general easterly direction, the western part only has cut for itself a cañon, while the eastern has formed a broad valley, called, in honor of an old-time trapper, Brown's Park,[2] and long known as a favorite winter resort for mountain men and Indians.

May 30.—This morning we are ready to enter the mysterious cañon, and start with some anxiety. The old mountaineers tell us that it cannot be run; the Indians say, "Water heap catch'em," but all are eager for the trial, and off we go.

---

[1] This turn to the southwest occurs in the midst of present-day Dinosaur National Monument, Colorado, at Steamboat Rock.
[2] In the 21st century, this contains the Browns Park National Wildlife Refuge, Colorado.

Entering Flaming Gorge, we quickly run through it on a swift current, and emerge into a little park. Half a mile below, the river wheels sharply to the left, and we turn into another cañon cut into the mountain. We enter the narrow passage. On either side, the walls rapidly increase in altitude. On the left are overhanging ledges and cliffs five hundred—a thousand—fifteen hundred feet high.

On the right, the rocks are broken and ragged, and the water fills the channel from cliff to cliff. Now the river turns abruptly around a point to the right, and the waters plunge swiftly down among great rocks; and here we have our first experience with cañon rapids. I stand up on the deck of my boat to seek a way among the wave beaten rocks. All untried as we are with such waters, the moments are filled with intense anxiety.

Soon our boats reach the swift current; a stroke or two, now on this side, now on that, and we thread the narrow passage with exhilarating velocity, mounting the high waves, whose foaming crests dash over us, and plunging into the troughs, until we reach the quiet water below; and then comes a feeling of great relief. Our first rapid is run. Another mile, and we come into the valley again.

Let me explain this cañon. Where the river turns to the left above, it takes a course directly into the mountain, penetrating to its very heart, then wheels back upon itself, and runs out into the valley from which it started only half a mile below the point at which it entered; so the cañon is in the form of an elongated letter U, with the apex in the center of the mountain. We name it Horseshoe cañon.[3]

Soon we leave the valley, and enter another short cañon, very narrow at first, but widening below as the cañon walls increase in height. Here we discover the mouth of a beautiful little creek, coming down through its narrow water worn cleft. Just at its entrance there is a park of two or three hundred acres, walled on every side by almost vertical cliffs, hundreds of feet in altitude, with three gateways through the walls—one up, another down the river,

---

[3] This is not the formation named Horseshoe Bend today, which was reached later in the expedition.

and a third passage through which the creek comes in. The river is broad, deep, and quiet, and its waters mirror towering rocks.

Kingfishers are playing about the streams, and so we adopt as names Kingfisher Creek, Kingfisher Park, and Kingfisher cañon. At night, we camp at the foot of this cañon.

Our general course this day has been south, but here the river turns to the east around a point which is rounded to the shape of a dome, and on its sides little cells have been carved by the action of the water; and in these pits, which cover the face of the dome, hundreds of swallows have built their nests. As they flit about the cliffs, they look like swarms of bees, giving to the whole the appearance of a colossal beehive of the old time form, and so we name it Beehive Point.

The opposite wall is a vast amphitheater, rising in a succession of terraces to a height of 1,200 or 1,500 feet. Each step is built of red sandstone, with a face of naked, red rock, and a glacis clothed with verdure. So the amphitheater seems banded red and green, and the evening sun is playing with roseate flashes on the rocks, with shimmering green on the cedars' spray, and iridescent gleams on the dancing waves. The landscape revels in the sunshine.

May 31.—We start down another cañon, and reach rapids made dangerous by high rocks lying in the channel; so we run ashore, and let our boats down with lines.[4] In the afternoon we come to more dangerous rapids, and stop to examine them. I find we must do the same work again, but, being on the wrong side of the river to obtain a foothold, must first cross over—no very easy matter in such a current, with rapids and rocks below. We take the pioneer boat *Emma Dean* over, and unload her on the hank; then she returns and takes another load. Running back and forth, she soon has half our cargo over; then one of the larger boats is manned and taken across, but carried down almost to the rocks in spite of hard rowing. The

---

[4] Lining the boats was extremely laborious work. They first had to be emptied and then "lined" downstream safely using ropes. Then the supplies had to be carried down and reloaded into the boats.

other boats follow and make the landing, and we go into camp for the night.

At the foot of the cliff on this side, there is a long slope covered with pines; under these we make our beds, and soon after sunset are seeking rest and sleep. The cliffs on either side are of red sandstone, and stretch up toward the heavens 2,500 feet. On this side, the long, pine clad slope is surmounted by perpendicular cliffs, with pines on their summits. The wall on the other side is bare rock from the water's edge up 2,000 feet, then slopes back, giving footing to pines and cedars.

As the twilight deepens, the rocks grow dark and somber; the threatening roar of the water is loud and constant, and I lie awake with thoughts of the morrow and the cañons to come, interrupted now and then by characteristics of the scenery that attract my attention. And here I make a discovery. On looking at the mountain directly in front, the steepness of the slope is greatly exaggerated, while the distance to its summit and its true altitude are correspondingly diminished. I have heretofore found that to properly judge of the slope of a mountain side, you must see it in profile. In coming down the river this afternoon, I observed the slope of a particular part of the wall, and made an estimate of its altitude. While at supper, I noticed the same cliff from a position facing it, and it seemed steeper, but not half as high. Now lying on my side and looking at it, the true proportions appear. This seems a wonder, and I rise up to take a view of it standing. It is the same cliff as at supper time. Lying down again, it is the cliff as seen in profile, with a long slope and distant summit. Musing on this, I forget "the morrow and the cañons to come."

I find a way to estimate the altitude and slope of an inclination as I can judge of distance along the horizon. The reason is simple. A reference to the stereoscope will suggest it. The distance between the eyes forms a base-line for optical triangulation.

June 1.—Today we have an exciting ride. The river rolls down the cañon at a wonderful rate, and, with no rocks in the way, we make almost railroad speed. Here and there the water rushes into a narrow gorge; the rocks on the side roll it into the center in great waves, and the boats go leaping and bounding over these like things of life. They remind me of scenes witnessed in Middle Park; herds of startled deer bounding through forests beset with fallen timber. I mention the resemblance to some of the hunters, and so striking is it that it comes to be a common expression, "See the black-tails jumping the logs." At times the waves break and roll over the boats, which necessitates much bailing, and obliges us to stop occasionally for that purpose. At one time, we run twelve miles an hour, stoppages included.

Last spring, I had a conversation with an old Indian named Pa'-ri-ats, who told me about one of his tribe attempting to run this cañon. "The rocks," he said, holding his hands above his head, his arms vertical, and looking between them to the heavens, "the rocks h-e-a-p, h-e-a-p high; the water go h-oo-woogh, h-oo-woogh; water-pony (boat) h-e-a-p buck; water catch'em; no see'em Injun anymore! no see'em squaw anymore! no see'em pappoose anymore!"

Those who have seen these wild Indian ponies rearing alternately before and behind, or "bucking," as it is called in the vernacular, will appreciate his description.

At last we come to calm water, and a threatening roar is heard in the distance. Slowly approaching the point whence the sound issues, we come near to falls, and tie up just above them on the left. Here we will be compelled to make a portage; so we unload the boats, and fasten a long line to the bow, and another to the stern, of the smaller one, and moor her close to the brink of the fall. Then the bow-line is taken below, and made fast; the stern-line is held by five or six men, and the boat let down as long as they can hold her against the rushing waters; then, letting go one end of the line, it runs through the ring; the boat leaps over the fall, and is caught by the lower rope.

Now we rest for the night.

June 2.—This morning we make a trail among the rocks, transport the cargoes to a point below the falls, let the remaining boats over, and are ready to start before noon.

On a high rock by which the trail passes we find the inscription: "Ashley 18–5." The third figure is obscure—some of the party reading it 1835, some 1855.[5]

James Baker, an old time mountaineer, once told me about a party of men starting down the river, and Ashley was named as one. The story runs that the boat was swamped, and some of the party drowned in one of the cañons below. The word "Ashley" is a warning to us, and we resolve on great caution.

Ashley Falls is the name we give to the cataract.

The river is very narrow; the right wall vertical for two or three hundred feet, the left towering to a great height, with a vast pile of broken rocks lying between the foot of the cliff and the water. Some of the rocks broken down from the ledge above have tumbled into the channel and caused this fall. One great cubical block, thirty or forty feet high, stands in the middle of the stream, and the waters, parting to either side, plunge down about twelve feet, and are broken again by the smaller rocks into a rapid below. Immediately below the falls, the water occupies the entire channel, there being no talus at the foot of the cliffs.

We embark, and run down a short distance, where we find a landing-place for dinner.

On the waves again all the afternoon. Near the lower end of this cañon, to which we have given the name Red cañon, is a little park, where streams come down from distant mountain summits, and enter the river on either side; and here we camp for the night under two stately pines.

June 3.—This morning we spread our rations, clothes, &c., on the ground to dry, and several of the party go out for a hunt. I take a walk of five or six miles up to a pine grove park, its grassy carpet bedecked with crimson, velvet flowers, set in groups on the stems of

---

[5] General Ashley, the fur trader, made his last journey into the Far West before 1835. The man here mentioned must have been someone else, of the same family name.—note by editor in original. Reference to William Henry Ashley (c. 1778–1838), who in 1835 was a member of the U.S. House of Representatives.

pear shaped cactus plants; patches of painted cups are seen here and there, with yellow blossoms protruding through scarlet bracts; little blue-eyed flowers are peeping through the grass; and the air is filled with fragrance from the white blossoms of a *Spiræa*. A mountain brook runs through the midst, ponded below by beaver dams. It is a quiet place for retirement from the raging waters of the cañon.

It will be remembered that the course of the river, from Flaming Gorge to Beehive Point, is in a southerly direction, and at right angles to the Uinta Mountains, and cuts into the range until it reaches a point within five miles of the crest, where it turns to the east, and pursues a course not quite parallel to the trend of the range, but crosses the axis slowly in a direction a little south of east. Thus there is a triangular tract between the river and the axis of the mountain, with its acute angle extending eastward. I climb a mountain overlooking this country. To the east, the peaks are not very high, and already most of the snow has melted; but little patches lie here and there under the lee of ledges of rock. To the west, the peaks grow higher and the snow fields larger. Between the brink of the cañon and the foot of these peaks, there is a high bench. A number of creeks have their sources in the snow banks to the south, and run north into the cañon, tumbling down from 3,000 to 5,000 feet in a distance of five or six miles. Along their upper courses, they run through grassy valleys; but, as they approach Red cañon, they rapidly disappear under the general surface of the country, and emerge into the cañon below in deep, dark gorges of their own. Each of these short lateral cañons is marked by a succession of cascades and a wild confusion of rocks and trees and fallen timber and thick undergrowth.

The little valleys above are beautiful parks; between the parks are stately pine forests, half hiding ledges of red sandstone. Mule-deer and elk abound; grizzly bears, too, are abundant; wild cats, wolverines, and mountain lions are here at home. The forest aisles are filled with the music of birds, and the parks are decked with flowers. Noisy brooks meander through them; ledges of moss-covered rocks are seen; and gleaming in the distance are the snow fields, and the mountain tops are away in the clouds.

June 4.—We start early and run through to Brown's Park. Half way down the valley, a spur of a red mountain stretches across the river, which cuts a cañon through it, Here the walls are comparatively low, but vertical. A vast number of swallows have built their adobe houses on the face of the cliffs, on either side of the river. The waters are deep and quiet, but the swallows are swift and noisy enough, sweeping by in their curved paths through the air, or chattering from the rocks. The young birds stretch their little heads on naked necks through the doorways of their mud houses, clamoring for food. They are a noisy people.

We call this Swallow cañon.

Still down the river we glide, until an early hour in the afternoon, when we go into camp under a giant cottonwood, standing on the right bank, a little way back from the stream. The party had succeeded in killing a fine lot of wild ducks, and during the afternoon a mess of fish is taken.

June 5.—With one of the men, I climb a mountain, off on the right. A long spur, with broken ledges of rocks, puts down to the river; and along its course, or up the "hog-back,'" as it is called, I make the ascent. Dunn, who is climbing to the same point, is coming up the gulch. Two hours' hard work has brought us to the summit. These mountains are all verdure clad; pine and cedar forests are set on green terraces; snow clad mountains are seen in the distance, to the west; the plains of the upper Breen stretch out before us, to the north, until they are lost in the blue heavens; but half of the river cleft range intervenes, and the river itself is at our feet.

This half range, beyond the river, is composed of long ridges, nearly parallel with the valley. On the farther ridge, to the north, four creeks have their sources. These cut through the intervening ridges, one of which is much higher than that on which they head, by cañon gorges; then they run, with gentle curves, across the valley, their banks set with willows, box-elders, and cottonwood groves.

To the east, we look up the valley of the Vermilion,[6] through which Fremont[7] found his path on his way to the great parks of Colorado.

The reading of the barometer taken, we start down in company, and reach camp tired and hungry, which does not abate one bit our enthusiasm, as we tell of the day's work, with its glory of landscape.

June 6.—At daybreak, I am awakened by a chorus of birds. It seems as if all the feathered songsters of the region have come to the old tree. Several species of warblers, woodpeckers, and flickers above, meadowlarks in the grass, and wild geese in the river. I recline on my elbow, and watch a lark nearby, and then awaken my bed fellow, to listen to my Jenny Lind.[8] A morning concert for me; none of your "matinees"

Our cook has been an ox-driver, or "bull-whacker," on the plains, in one of those long trains now no longer seen, and he hasn't forgotten his old ways. In the midst of the concert, his voice breaks in: "Roll out! roll out! bulls in the corral! chain up the gaps! Roll out! roll out! roll out!" And this is our breakfast bell. Today we pass through the park, and camp at the head of another cañon.

June 7.—today, two or three of us climb to the summit of the cliff, on the left, and find its altitude, above camp, to be 2,086 feet. The rocks are split with fissures, deep and narrow, sometimes a hundred feet, or more, to the bottom. Lofty pines find root in the fissures that are filled with loose earth and decayed vegetation. On a rock we find a pool of clear, cold water, caught from yesterday evening's shower. After a good drink, we walk out to the brink of the cañon, and look down to the water below. I can do this now, but it has taken several years of mountain climbing to cool my nerves, so that I can sit, with my feet over the edge, and calmly look down a precipice 2,000 feet.

And yet I cannot look on and see another do the same. I must either bid him come away, or turn my head.

---

[6] Vermillion Creek enters the Green River about 2.6 miles by river from the present day Lodore Ranger Station within the Browns Park National Wildlife Refuge.—2020

[7] General John C. Frémont (1813–1890), politician, explorer, and soldier known as The Pathfinder.

[8] Powell is making an allusion between his feathered friend and the great 19th century Swedish opera singer, Jenny Lind (1820–1887).

The cañon walls are buttressed on a grand scale, with deep alcoves intervening; columned crags crown the cliffs, and the river is rolling below.

When we return to camp, at noon, the sun shines in splendor on vermilion walls, shaded into green and gray, where the rocks are lichened over; the river fills the channel from wall to wall, and the cañon opens, like a beautiful portal, to a region of glory.

This evening, as I write, the sun is going down, and the shadows are settling in the cañon. The vermilion gleams and roseate hues, blending with the green and gray tints, are slowly changing to somber brown above, and black shadows are creeping over them below; and now it is a dark portal to a region of gloom—the gateway through which we are to enter on our voyage of exploration tomorrow. What shall we find?

The distance from Flaming Gorge to Beehive Point is nine and two-thirds miles. Besides, passing through the gorge, the river runs through Horseshoe and Kingfisher cañons, separated by short valleys. The highest point on the walls, at Flaming Gorge, is 1,300 feet above the river. The east wall, at the apex of Horseshoe cañon, is about 1,600 feet above the water's edge, and, from this point, the walls slope both to the head and foot of the cañon.

Kingfisher cañon, starting at the water's edge above, steadily increases in altitude to 1,200 feet at the foot.

Red cañon is twenty-five and two-thirds miles long, and the highest walls are about 2,500 feet.

Brown's Park is a valley, bounded on either side by a mountain range, really an expansion of the cañon. The river, through the park, is thirty-five and a half miles long, but passes through two short cañons, on its way, where spurs, from the mountains on the south, are thrust across its course.

THE CANYON OF LODORE

JUNE 8.—We enter the cañon, and, until noon, find a succession of rapids, over which our boats have to be taken.

Here I must explain our method of proceeding at such places. The *Emma Dean* goes in advance; the other boats follow, in obedience to signals. When we approach a rapid, or what, on other rivers, would often be called a fall, I stand on deck to examine it, while the oarsmen back water, and we drift on as slowly as possible. If I can see a clear chute between the rocks, away we go; but if the channel is beset entirely across, we signal the other boats, pull to land, and I walk along the shore for closer examination. If this reveals no clear channel, hard work begins. We drop the boats to the very head of the dangerous place, and let them over by lines, or make a portage, frequently carrying both boats and cargoes over the rocks, or, perhaps, only the cargoes, if it is safe to let the boats down.

The waves caused by such falls in a river differ much from the waves of the sea. The water of an ocean wave merely rises and falls; the form only passes on, and form chases form unceasingly. A body floating on such waves merely rises and sinks—does not progress unless impelled by wind or some other power. But here, the water of the wave passes on, while the form remains. The waters plunge down ten or twenty feet, to the foot of a fall; spring up again in a great wave; then down and up, in a series of billows, that gradually disappear in the more quiet waters below; but these waves are always there, and you can stand above and count them.

A boat riding such, leaps and plunges along with great velocity. Now, the difficulty in riding over these falls, when the rocks are out of the way, is in the first wave at the foot. This will sometimes gather for a moment, heaping up higher and higher, until it breaks back. If the boat strikes it the instant after it breaks, she cuts through, and the mad breaker dashes its spray over the boat, and would wash us overboard did we not cling tight. If the boat, in going over the falls, chances to get caught in some side current, and is turned from its course, so as to strike the wave "broadside on," and the wave breaks at the same instant, the boat is capsized. Still, we must cling to her, for, the water tight compartments acting as buoys, she cannot sink; and so we go, dragged through the waves, until still waters are reached. We then right the boat, and climb aboard. We have several such experiences today.

At night, we camp on the right bank, on a little shelving rock, between the river and the foot of the cliff; and with night comes gloom into these great depths.

After supper, we sit by our camp fire, made of driftwood caught by the rocks, and tell stories of wild life; for the men have seen such in the mountains, or on the plains, and on the [Civil War] battlefields of the South. It is late before we spread our blankets on the beach.

Lying down, we look up through the cañon, and see that only a little of the blue heaven appears overhead—a crescent of blue sky, with two or three constellations peering down upon us.

I do not sleep for some time, as the excitement of the day has not worn off. Soon I see a bright star that appears to rest on the very verge of the cliff overhead to the east. Slowly it seems to float from its resting place on the rock over the cañon. At first, it appears like a jewel set on the brink of the cliff; but, as it moves out from the rock, I almost wonder that it does not fall. In fact, it does seem to descend in a gentle curve, as though the bright sky in which the stars are set was spread across the cañon, resting on either wall, and swayed down by its own weight. The stars appear to be in the cañon. I soon discover that it is the bright star Vega, so it occurs to me to designate this part of the wall as the "Cliff of the Harp"

June 9.—One of the party suggests that we call this the cañon of Lodore, and the name is adopted.[1] Very slowly we make our way, often climbing on the rocks at the edge of the water for a few hundred yards, to examine the channel before running it.

---

[1] The name persists in the 21st century and is an extremely popular rafting destination. *Lodore* is a work by English Romantic novelist Mary Shelley (author of *Frankenstein*), completed in 1833 and published in 1835.

During the afternoon, we come to a place where it is necessary to make a portage. The little boat is landed, and the others are signaled to come up.

When these rapids or broken falls occur, usually the channel is suddenly narrowed by rocks which have been tumbled from the cliffs or have been washed in by lateral streams. Immediately above the narrow, rocky channel, on one or both sides, there is often a bay of quiet water, in which we can land with ease. Sometimes the water descends with a smooth, unruffled surface, from the broad, quiet spread above, into the narrow, angry channel below, by a semicircular sag. Great care must be taken not to pass over the brink into this deceptive pit, but above it we can row with safety. I walk along the bank to examine the ground, leaving one of my men with a flag to guide the other boats to the landing-place. I soon see one of the boats make shore all right and feel no more concern; but a minute after, I hear a shout, and looking around, see one of the boats shooting down the center of the sag. It is the *No Name*, with Captain Howland, his brother, and Goodman. I feel that its going over is inevitable, and run to save the third boat. A minute more, and she turns the point and heads for the shore. Then I turn down stream again, and scramble along to look for the boat that has gone over. The first fall is not great, only ten or twelve feet, and we often run such; but below, the river tumbles down again for forty or fifty feet, in a channel filled with dangerous rocks that break the waves into whirlpools and beat them into foam. I pass around a great crag just in time to see the boat strike a rock, and, rebounding from the shock, careen and fill the open compartment with water. Two of the men lose their oars; she swings around, and is carried down at a rapid rate, broadside on, for a few yards, and strikes amidships on another rock with great force, is broken quite in two, and the men are thrown into the river; the larger part of the boat floating buoyantly, they soon seize it, and down the river they drift, past the rocks for a few hundred yards to a second rapid, filled with huge boulders, where the boat strikes again, and is dashed to pieces, and the men and fragments are soon carried beyond my sight. Running along, I turn a bend, and see a man's head above the water, washed about in a whirlpool below a great rock.

29

It is Frank Goodman, clinging to it with a grip upon which life depends. Coming opposite, I see Howland trying to go to his aid from an island on which he has been washed. Soon, he comes near enough to reach Frank with a pole, which he extends toward him. The latter lets go the rock, grasps the pole, and is pulled ashore. Seneca Howland is washed farther down the island, and is caught by some rocks, and, though somewhat bruised, manages to get ashore in safety. This seems a long time, as I tell it, but it is quickly done.

And now the three men are on an island, with a swift, dangerous river on either side and a fall below. The *Emma Dean* is soon brought down, and Sumner, starting above as far as possible, pushes out. Right skillfully he plies the oars, and a few strokes set him on the island at the proper point. Then they all pull the boat up stream, as far as they are able, until they stand in water up to their necks. One sits on a rock, and holds the boat until the others are ready to pull, then gives the boat a push, clings to it with his hands, and climbs in as they pull for mainland, which they reach in safety. We are as glad to shake hands with them as though they had been on a voyage around the world, and wrecked on a distant coast.

Down the river half a mile we find that the after cabin of the wrecked boat, with a part of the bottom, ragged and splintered, has floated against a rock, and stranded. There are valuable articles in the cabin; but, on examination, we determine that life should not be risked to save them. Of course, the cargo of rations, instruments, and clothing is gone.

We return to the boats, and make camp for the night. No sleep comes to me in all those dark hours. The rations, instruments, and clothing have been divided among the boats, anticipating such an accident as this; and we started with duplicates of everything that was deemed necessary to success. But, in the distribution, there was one exception to this precaution, and the barometers were all placed in one boat, and they are lost. There is a possibility that they are in the cabin lodged against the rock, for that is where they were kept. But, then, how to reach them! The river is rising. Will they be there tomorrow? Can I go out to Salt Lake City, and obtain barometers from New York?

June 10.—I have determined to get the barometers from the wreck, if they are there. After breakfast, while the men make the portage, I go down again for another examination. There the cabin lies, only carried fifty or sixty feet farther on.

Carefully looking over the ground, I am satisfied that it can be reached with safety, and return to tell the men my conclusion. Sumner and Dunn volunteer to take the little boat and make the attempt. They start, reach it, and out come the barometers; and now the boys set up a shout, and I join them, pleased that they should be as glad to save the instruments as myself. When the boat lands on our side, I find that the only things saved from the wreck were the barometers, a package of thermometers, and a three gallon keg of whisky, which is what the men were shouting about. They had taken it aboard, unknown to me, and now I am glad they did, for they think it will do them good, as they are drenched every day by the melting snow, which runs down the summits of the Rocky Mountains.

Now we come back to our work at the portage. We find that it is necessary to carry our rations over the rocks for nearly a mile, and let our boats down with lines, except at a few points, where they also must be carried.

Between the river and the eastern wall of the cañon there is an immense talus of broken rocks. These have tumbled down from the cliffs above, and constitute a vast pile of huge angular fragments. On these we build a path for a quarter of a mile, to a small sand beach covered with drift-wood, through which we clear a way for several hundred yards, then continue the trail on over another pile of rocks, nearly half a mile farther down, to a little bay. The greater part of the day is spent in this work. Then we carry our cargoes down to the beach and camp for the night.

While the men are building the camp fire, we discover an iron bake oven, several tin plates, a part of a boat, and many other fragments, which denote that this is the place where Ashley's party was wrecked.

June 11.—This day is spent in carrying our rations down to the bay—no small task to climb over the rocks with sacks of flour or bacon. We carry them by stages of about 500 yards each, and when night comes, and the last sack is on the beach, we are tired, bruised, and glad to sleep.

June 12.—Today we take the boats down to the bay. While at this work, we discover three sacks of flour from the wrecked boat that have lodged in the rocks. We carry them above high-water mark, and leave them, as our cargoes are already too heavy for the three remaining boats. We also find two or three oars, which we place with them.

As Ashley and his party were wrecked here, and as we have lost one of our boats at the same place, we adopt the name Disaster Falls for the scene of so much peril and loss.

Though some of his companions were drowned, Ashley and one other survived the wreck, climbed the cañon wall, and found their way across the Wasatch Mountains to Salt Lake City, living chiefly on berries, as they wandered through an unknown and difficult country. When they arrived at Salt Lake, they were almost destitute of clothing, and nearly starved. The Mormon people gave them food and clothing, and employed them to work on the foundation of the Temple, until they had earned sufficient to enable them to leave the country. Of their subsequent history, I have no knowledge. It is possible they returned to the scene of the disaster, as a little creek entering the river below is known as Ashley's Creek, and it is reported that he built a cabin and trapped on this river for one or two winters; but this may have been before the disaster.

June 13.—Still rocks, rapids, and portages.

We camp tonight at the foot of the left wall on a little patch of flood-plain covered with a dense growth of box-elders, stopping early in order to spread the clothing and rations to dry. Everything is wet and spoiling.

June 14.—Howland and I climb the wall, on the west side of the cañon, to an altitude of 2,000 feet. Standing above, and looking to the west, we discover a large park, five or six miles wide and twenty or thirty long. The cliff we have climbed forms a wall between the cañon and the park, for it is 800 feet, down the western side, to the valley. A creek comes winding down, 1,200 feet above the river, and, entering the intervening wall by a cañon, it plunges down, more than a thousand feet, by a broken cascade, into the river below.

June 15.—Today, while we make another portage, a peak, standing on the east wall, is climbed by two of the men, and found to be 2,700 feet above the river. On the east side of the cañon, a vast amphitheater has been cut, with massive buttresses, and deep, dark alcoves, in which grow beautiful mosses and delicate ferns, while springs burst out from the further recesses, and wind, in silver threads, over floors of sand rock. Here we have three falls in close succession. At the first, the water is compressed into a very narrow channel, against the right-hand cliff, and falls fifteen feet in ten yards; at the second, we have a broad sheet of water, tumbling down twenty feet over a group of rocks that thrust their dark heads through the foaming waters. The third is a broken fall, or short, abrupt rapid, where the water makes a descent of more than twenty feet among huge, fallen fragments of the cliff. We name the group Triplet Falls.[2] We make a portage around the first; past the second and third we let down with lines.

During the afternoon, Dunn and Howland, having returned from their climb, we run down, three-quarters of a mile, on quiet water, and land at the head of another fall. On examination, we find that there is an abrupt plunge of a few feet, and then the river tumbles, for half a mile, with a descent of a hundred feet, in a channel beset with great numbers of huge boulders. This stretch of the river is named Hell's Half-Mile.

The remaining portion of the day is occupied in making a trail among the rocks to the foot of the rapid.

June 16.—Our first work this morning is to carry our cargoes to the foot of the falls, Then we commence letting down the boats. We take two of them down in safety, but not without great difficulty; for, where such a vast body of water, rolling down an inclined plane, is

---

[2] Still marked with this name on 21st century maps of Colorado.

33

broken into eddies and cross currents by rocks projecting from the cliffs and piles of boulders in the channel, it requires excessive labor and much care to prevent their being dashed against the rocks or breaking away. Sometimes we are compelled to hold the boat against a rock, above a chute, until a second line, attached to the stem, is carried to some point below, and, when all is ready, the first line is detached, and the boat given to the current, when she shoots down, and the men below swing her into some eddy.

At such a place, we are letting down the last boat, and, as she is set free, a wave turns her broadside down the stream, with the stem, to which the line is attached, from shore, and a little up. They haul on the line to bring the boat in, but the power of the current, striking obliquely against her, shoots her out into the middle of the river. The men have their hands burned with the friction of the passing line; the boat breaks away, and speeds, with great velocity, down the stream.

The *Maid of the cañon* is lost, so it seems; but she drifts some distance, and swings into an eddy, in which she spins about, until we arrive with the small boat, and rescue her.

Soon we are on our way again, and stop at the mouth of a little brook, on the right, for a late dinner. This brook comes down from the distant mountains, in a deep side cañon. We set out to explore it, but are soon cut off from farther progress up the gorge by a high rock, over which the brook glides in a smooth sheet. The rock is not quite vertical, and the water does not plunge over in a fall.

Then we climb up to the left for an hour, and are a thousand feet above the river, and six hundred above the brook. Just before us, the cañon divides, a little stream coming down on the right, and another on the left, and we can look away up either of these cañons, through an ascending vista, to cliffs and crags and towers, a mile back, and two thousand feet overhead. To the right, a dozen gleaming cascades are seen. Pines and firs stand on the rocks and aspens overhang the brooks. The rocks below are red and brown, set in deep shadows, but above, they are buff and vermilion, and stand in the sunshine. The light above, made more brilliant by the bright-tinted rocks, and the shadows below more gloomy by the somber hues of the brown walls, increase the apparent depths of the cañons, and it seems a long way up to the world of sunshine and open sky, and a long way down to the bottom of the cañon glooms. Never before have I received such an impression of the vast heights of these cañon walls; not even at the Cliff of the Harp, where the very heavens seemed to rest on their summits.

We sit on some overhanging rocks, and enjoy the scene for a time, listening to the music of falling waters away up the cañons. We name this Rippling Brook.[3]

Late in the afternoon we make a short run to the mouth of another little creek, coming down from the left into an alcove filled with luxuriant vegetation. Here camp is made with a group of cedars on one side and a dense mass of box-elders and dead willows on the other.

I go up to explore the alcove. While away a whirlwind comes, scattering the fire among the dead willows and cedar-spray, and soon there is a conflagration. The men rush for the boats, leaving all they cannot readily seize at the moment, and even then they have their clothing burned and hair singed, and Bradley has his ears scorched. The cook fills his arms with the mess-kit, and, jumping into a boat, stumbles and falls, and away go our cooking utensils into the river. Our plates are gone; our spoons are gone; our knives and forks are gone. "Water catch'em; h-e-a-p catch em."

When on the boats, the men are compelled to cut loose, as the flames, running out on the overhanging willows, are scorching them. Loose on the stream, they must go down, for the water is too swift to make headway against it. Just below is a rapid, filled with rocks. On they shoot, no channel explored, no signal to guide them. Just at this juncture I chance to see them, but have not yet discovered the fire, and the strange movements of the men fill me with astonishment. Down the rocks I clamber, and run to the bank. When I arrive, they have landed. Then we all go back to the late camp to see if anything left behind can be saved. Some of the clothing and

---

[3] This small watercourse retains this name in the 21st century and enters the Green River from the west.

bedding taken out of the boats is found, also a few tin cups, basins, and a camp kettle, and this is all the mess kit we now have. Yet we do just as well as ever.

June 17.—We run down to the mouth of Yampa River.[4] This has been a chapter of disasters and toils, notwithstanding which the cañon of Lodore was not devoid of scenic interest, even beyond the power of pen to tell. The roar of its waters was heard unceasingly from the hour we entered it until we landed here. No quiet in all that time. But its walls and cliffs, its peaks and crags, its amphitheaters and alcoves, tell a story of beauty and grandeur that I hear yet—and shall hear.

The cañon of Lodore is twenty and three-quarter miles in length. It starts abruptly at what we have called the Gate of Lodore, with walls nearly two thousand feet high, and they are never lower than this until we reach Alcove Brook, about three miles above the foot. They are very irregular, standing in vertical or overhanging cliffs in places, terraced in others, or receding in steep slopes, and are broken by many side gulches and cañons. The highest point on the wall is at Dunn's Cliff, near Triplet Falls, where the rocks reach an altitude of 2,700 feet, but the peaks a little way back rise nearly a thousand feet higher. Yellow pines, nut pines, firs, and cedars stand in extensive forests on the Uinta Mountains, and, clinging to the rocks and growing in the crevices, come down the walls to the water's edge from Flaming Gorge to Echo Park. The red sandstones are lichened over; delicate mosses grow in the moist places, and ferns festoon the walls.

---

4 The confluence of the Green and Yampa Rivers is now a historical landmark.

FROM ECHO PARK TO THE MOUTH OE THE UINTA RIYER

THE Yampa enters the Green from the east. At a point opposite its mouth, the Green runs to the south, at the foot of a rock, about seven hundred feet high and a mile long, and then turns sharply around it to the right, and runs back in a northerly course, parallel to its former direction, for nearly another mile, thus having the opposite sides of a long, narrow rock for its bank. The tongue of rock so formed is a peninsular precipice, with a mural escarpment along its whole course on the east, but broken down at places on the west.

On the east side of the river, opposite the rock, and below the Yampa, there is a little park, just large enough for a farm, already; fenced with high walls of gray homogeneous sandstone. There are three river entrances to this park: one down the Yampa; one below, by coming up the Green; and another down the Green. There is also a land entrance down a lateral cañon. Elsewhere the park is inaccessible. Through this land-entrance by the side cañon there is a trail made by Indian hunters, who come down here in certain seasons to kill mountain sheep.

Great hollow domes are seen in the eastern side of the rock, against which the Green sweeps; willows border the river; clumps of box-elder are seen; and a few cottonwoods stand at the lower end. Standing opposite the rock, our words are repeated with startling clearness, but in a soft, mellow tone, that transforms them into magical music. Scarcely can you believe it is the echo of your own voice. In some places two or three echoes come back; in other places they; repeat themselves, passing back and forth across the river between this rock and the eastern wall.

To hear these repeated echoes well you must shout. Some of the party aver that ten or twelve repetitions can be heard. To me, they seem to rapidly diminish and merge by multiplicity, like telegraph poles on an outstretched plain. I have observed the same phenomenon once before in the cliffs near Long's Peak, and am pleased to meet with it again.

During the afternoon, Bradley and I climb some cliffs to the north. Mountain sheep are seen above us, and they stand out on the rocks, and eye us intently, not seeming to move. Their color is much like that of the gray sandstone beneath them, and, immovable as they are, they appear like carved forms. Now a fine ram beats the rock with his front foot, and, wheeling around, they all bound away together, leaping over rocks and chasms, and climbing walls where no man can follow, and this with an ease and gracefulness most wonderful. At night we return to our camp, under the box-elders, by the river side. Here we are to spend two or three days, making a series of astronomic observations for latitude and longitude.

June 18.—We have named the long peninsular rock on the other side Echo Rock.[1] Desiring to climb it, Bradley and I take the little boat and pull up stream as far as possible, for it cannot be climbed directly opposite. We land on a talus of rocks at the upper end, to reach a place where it seems practicable to make the ascent; but we must go still farther up the river. So we scramble along, until we reach a place where the river sweeps against the wall. Here we find a shelf, along which we can pass, and now are ready for the climb.

We start up a gulch; then pass to the left, on a bench, along the wall; then up again, over broken rocks; then we reach more benches, along which we walk, until we find more broken rocks and crevices, by which we climb still up, until we have ascended six or eight hundred feet; then we are met by a sheer precipice.

Looking about, we find a place where it seems possible to climb. I go ahead; Bradley hands the barometer to me, and follows. So we proceed, stage by stage, until we are nearly to the summit. Here, by making a spring, I gain a foothold in a little crevice, and grasp an angle of the rock overhead. I find I can get up no farther, and cannot step back, for I dare not let go with my hand, and cannot reach foothold below without. I call to Bradley for help. He finds a way by which he can get to the top of the rock over my head, but cannot reach me. Then he looks around for some stick or limb of a tree, but finds none. Then he suggests that he had better help me with the barometer case; but I fear I cannot hold on to it. The moment is critical. Standing on my toes, my muscles begin to tremble. It is sixty

---

[1] Now called Steamboat Rock.

or eighty feet to the foot of the precipice. If I lose my hold I shall fall to the bottom, and then perhaps roll over the bench, and tumble still farther down the cliff. At this instant it occurs to Bradley to take off his drawers, which he does, and swings them down to me. I hug close to the rock, let go with my hand, seize the dangling legs, and, with his assistance, I am enabled to gain the top.

Then we walk out on a peninsular rock, make the necessary observations for determining its altitude above camp, and return, finding an easy way down.

June 19.—Today, Howland, Bradley, and I take the *Emma Dean*, and start up the Yampa River. The stream is much swollen, the current swift, and we are able to make but slow progress against it. The cañon in this part of the course of the Yampa is cut through light gray sandstone. The river is very winding, and the swifter water is usually found on the outside of the curve, sweeping against vertical cliffs, often a thousand feet high. In the center of these curves, in many places, the rock above overhangs the river. On the opposite side, the walls are broken, craggy, and sloping, and occasionally side cañons enter. When we have rowed until we are quite tired we stop, and take advantage of one of these broken places to climb out of the cañon. When above, we can look up the Yampa for a distance of several miles.

From the summit of the immediate walls of the cañon the rocks rise gently back for a distance of a mile or two, having the appearance of a valley, with an irregular, rounded sandstone floor, and in the center of the valley a deep gorge, which is the cañon. The rim of this valley on the north is from two thousand five hundred to three thousand feet above the river; on the south, it is not so high. A number of peaks stand on this northern rim, the highest of which has received the name Mount Dawes.

Late in the afternoon we descend to our boat, and return to camp in Echo Park, gliding down in twenty minutes on the rapid river a distance of four or five miles, which was only made up stream by several hours' hard rowing in the morning.

39

June 20.—This morning two of the men take me up the Yampa for a short distance, and I go out to climb. Having reached the top of the cañon, I walk over long stretches of naked sandstone, crossing gulches now and then, and by noon reach the summit of Mount Dawes.[2] From this point I can look away to the north, and see in the dim distance the Sweetwater and Wind River Mountains, more than a hundred miles away. To the northwest, the Wasatch Mountains are in view and peaks of the Uinta. To the east, I can see the western slopes of the Rocky Mountains, more than a hundred and fifty miles distant.

The air is singularly clear today; mountains and buttes stand in sharp outline, valleys stretch out in the perspective, and I can look down into the deep cañon gorges and see gleaming waters.

Descending, I cross a ridge near the brink of the cañon of Lodore, the highest point of which is nearly as high as the last mentioned mountain.

Late in the afternoon I stand on this elevated point, and discover a monument that has evidently been built by human hands. A few plants are growing in the joints between the rocks, and all are lichened over to a greater or less extent, showing evidences that the pile was built a long time ago. This line of peaks, the eastern extension of the Uinta Mountains, has received the name of Sierra Escalanti, in honor of a Spanish priest, who traveled in this region of country nearly a century ago; and, perchance, the reverend father built this monument.

Now I return to the river and discharge my gun, as a signal for the boat to come and take me down to camp. While we have been in the park, the men have succeeded in catching quite a number of fish, and we have an abundant supply. This is quite an addition to our cuisine.

June 21.—We float around the long rock, and enter another cañon. The walls are high and vertical; the cañon is narrow; and the river fills the whole space below, so that there is no landing-place at the

---

[2] There is no feature in the vicinity with this name in the 21st century.

foot of the cliff. The Green is greatly increased by the Yampa, and we now have a much larger river. All this volume of water, confined, as it is, in a narrow channel, and rushing with great velocity, is set eddying and spinning in whirlpools by projecting rocks and short curves, and the waters waltz their way through the cañon, making their own rippling, rushing, roaring music. The cañon is much narrower than any we have seen. With difficulty we manage our boats. They spin about from side to side, and we know not where we are going, and find it impossible to keep them headed down the stream. At first, this causes us great alarm, but we soon find there is but little danger, and that there is a general movement of progression down the river, to which this whirling is but an adjunct; and it is the merry mood of the river to dance through this deep, dark gorge; and right gaily do we join in the sport.

Soon our revel is interrupted by a cataract; its roaring command is heeded by all our power at the oars, and we pull against the whirling current. The *Emma Dean* is brought up against a cliff, about fifty feet above the brink of the fall. By vigorously plying the oars on the side opposite the wall, as if to pull up stream, we can hold her against the rock. The boats behind are signaled to land where they can. The *Maid of the cañon* is pulled to the left wall, and, by constant rowing, they can hold her also. The *Sister* is run into an alcove on the right, where an eddy is in a dance, and in this she joins. Now my little boat is held against the wall only by the utmost exertion, and it is impossible to make headway against the current. On examination, I find a horizontal crevice in the rock, about ten feet above the water, and a boat's length below us, so we let her down to that point. One of the men clambers into the crevice, in which he can just crawl; we toss him the line, which he makes fast in the rocks, and now our boat is tied up. Then I follow into the crevice, and we crawl along a distance of fifty feet, or more, upstream, and find a broken place, where we can climb about fifty feet higher. Here we stand on a shelf that passes along downstream to a point above the falls, where it is broken down, and a pile of rocks, over which we can descend to the river, is lying against the foot of the cliff.

It has been mentioned that one of the boats is on the other side. I signal for the men to pull her up alongside of the wall, but it cannot be done; then to cross. This they do, gaining the wall on our side just above where the *Emma Dean* is tied.

The third boat is out of sight, whirling in the eddy of a recess. Looking about, I find another horizontal crevice, along which I crawl to a point just over the water, where this boat is lying, and, calling loud and long, I finally succeed in making the crew understand that I want them to bring the boat down, hugging the wall. This they accomplish, by taking advantage of every crevice and knob on the face of the cliff, so that we have the three boats together at a point a few yards above the falls. Now, by passing a line up on the shelf, the boats can be let down to the broken rocks below. This we do, and, making a short portage, our troubles here are over.

Below the falls, the cañon is wider, and there is more or less space between the river and the walls; but the stream, though wide, is rapid, and rolls at a fearful rate among the rocks. We proceed with great caution, and run the large boats altogether by signal.

At night we camp at the mouth of a small creek, which affords us a good supper of trout. In camp, tonight, we discuss the propriety of several different names for this cañon. At the falls, encountered at noon, its characteristics change suddenly. Above, it is very narrow, and the walls are almost vertical; below, the cañon is much wider, and more flaring; and, high up on the sides, crags, pinnacles, and towers are seen. A number of wild, narrow side cañons enter, and the walls are much broken. After many suggestions, our choice rests between two names, Whirlpool cañon[3] and Craggy cañon, neither of which is strictly appropriate for both parts of it; but we leave the discussion at this point, with the understanding that it is best, before finally deciding on a name, to wait until we see what the cañon is below.

June 22.—Still making short portages and letting down with lines. While we are waiting for dinner today, I climb a point that gives me

---

[3] A feature in this general vicinity is named Whirlpool Canyon in the 21st century.

a good view of the river for two or three miles below, and I think we can make a long run. After dinner, we start; the large boats are to follow in fifteen minutes, and look out for the signal to land. Into the middle of the stream we row, and down the rapid river we glide, only making strokes enough with the oars to guide the boat. What a headlong ride it is! shooting past rocks and islands! I am soon filled with exhilaration only experienced before in riding a fleet horse over the outstretched prairie. One, two, three, four miles we go, rearing and plunging with the waves, until we wheel to the right into a beautiful park, and land on an island, where we go into camp.

An hour or two before sunset, I cross to the mainland, and climb a point of rocks where I can overlook the park and its surroundings. On the east it is bounded by a high mountain ridge. A semicircle of naked hills bounds it on the north, west, and south. The broad, deep river meanders through the park, interrupted by many wooded islands; so I name it Island Park,[4] and decide to call the cañon above Whirlpool cañon.

June 23.—We remain in camp today to repair our boats, which have had hard knocks, and are leaking. Two of the men go out with the barometer to climb the cliff at the foot of Whirlpool cañon and measure the walls; another goes on the mountain to hunt; and Bradley and I spend the day among the rocks, studying an interesting geological fold and collecting fossils. Late in the afternoon, the hunter returns, and brings with him a fine, fat deer, so we give his name to the mountain—Mount Hawkins. Just before night we move camp to the lower end of the park, floating down the river about four miles.

June 24.—Bradley and I start early to climb the mountain ridge to the east; find its summit to be nearly three thousand feet above camp, and it has required some labor to scale it; but on its top, what a view! There is a long spur running out from the Uinta Mountains toward the south, and the river runs lengthwise through it. Coming down Lodore and Whirlpool cañons, we cut through the southern

---

[4] Many of the names Powell lists are retained today and their locations are easily found with online maps.

43

slope of the Uinta Mountains; and the lower end of this latter cañon runs into the spur, but, instead of splitting it the whole length, the river wheels to the right at the foot of Whirlpool cañon, in a great curve to the northwest, through Island Park. At the lower end of the park, the river turns again to the southeast, and cuts into the mountain to its center, and then makes a detour to the southwest, splitting the mountain ridge for a distance of six miles nearly to its foot, and then turns out of it to the left. All this we can see where we stand on the summit of Mount Hawkins, and so we name the gorge below Split Mountain cañon.

We are standing three thousand feet above its waters, which are troubled with billows, and white with foam. Its walls are set with crags and peaks, and buttressed towers, and overhanging domes. Turning to the right, the park is below us, with its island groves reflected by the deep, quiet waters. Rich meadows stretch out on either hand, to the verge of a sloping plain that comes down from the distant mountains. These plains are of almost naked rock, in strange contrast to the meadows; blue and lilac colored rocks, buff and pink, vermilion and brown, and all these colors clear and bright. A dozen little creeks, dry the greater part of the year, run down through the half circle of exposed formations, radiating from the island-center to the rim of the basin. Each creek has its system of side streams, and each side stream has its system of laterals, and, again, these are divided, so that this outstretched slope of rock is elaborately embossed. Beds of different colored formations run in parallel bands on either side. The perspective, modified by the undulations, gives the bands a waved appearance, and the high colors gleam in the midday sun with the luster of satin. We are tempted to call this Rainbow Park. Away beyond these beds are the Uinta and Wasatch Mountains, with their pine forests and snow fields and naked peaks. Now we turn to the right, and look up Whirlpool cañon, a deep gorge, with a river in the bottom—a gloomy chasm, where mad waves roar; but, at this distance and altitude, the river is but a rippling brook, and the chasm a narrow cleft. The top of the mountain on which we stand is a broad, grassy table, and a herd of deer is feeding in the distance. Walking over to the southeast, we look down into the valley of White River, and beyond

44

that see the far distant Rocky Mountains, in mellow, perspective haze, through which snow fields shine.

June 25.—This morning, we enter Split Mountain cañon, sailing in through a broad, flaring, brilliant gateway. We run two or three rapids after they have been carefully examined. Then we have a series of six or eight, over which we are compelled to pass by letting the boats down with lines. This occupies the entire day, and we camp at night at the mouth of a great cave.

The cave is at the foot of one of these rapids, and the waves dash in nearly to its very end. We can pass along a little shelf at the side until we reach the back part. Swallows have built their nests in the ceiling, and they wheel in, chattering and scolding at our intrusion; but their clamor is almost drowned by the noise of the waters. Looking out of the cave, we can see, far up the river, a line of crags standing sentinel on either side, and Mount Hawkins in the distance.

June 26.—The forenoon is spent in getting our large boats over the rapids. This afternoon, we find three falls in close succession. We carry our rations over the rocks, and let our boats shoot over the falls, checking and bringing them to land with lines in the eddies below. At three o'clock we are all aboard again. Down the river we are carried by the swift waters at great speed, sheering around a rock now and then with a timely stroke or two of the oars. At one point, the river turns from left to right, in a direction at right angles to the cañon, in a long chute, and strikes the right, where its waters are heaped up in great billows, that tumble back in breakers. We glide into the chute before we see the danger, and it is too late to stop. Two or three hard strokes are given on the right, and we pause for an instant, expecting to be dashed against the rock. The bow of the boat leaps high on a great wave; the rebounding waters hurl us back, and the peril is past. The next moment, the other boats are hurriedly signaled to land on the left. Accomplishing this, the men walk along the shore, holding the boats near the bank, and let them drift around. Starting again, we soon debouch into a beautiful valley, and glide down its length for ten miles, and camp under a grand old cottonwood. This is evidently a frequent resort for Indians. Tent poles are lying about, and the dead embers of late camp fires are seen. On the plains, to the left, antelope are feeding. Now and then a wolf is seen, and after dark they make the air resound with their howling.

June 27.—Now our way is along a gently flowing river, beset with many islands; groves are seen on either side, and natural meadows, where herds of antelope are feeding. Here and there we have views of the distant mountains on the right.

During the afternoon, we make a long detour to the west, and return again, to a point not more than half a mile from where we started at noon, and here we camp, for the night, under a high bluff.

June 28.—today, the scenery on either side of the river is much the same as that of yesterday, except that two or three lakes are discovered, lying in the valley to the west. After dinner, we run but a few minutes, when we discover the mouth of the Uinta, a river coming in from the west. Up the valley of this stream, about forty miles, the reservation of the Uinta Indians is situated. We propose to go there, and see if we can replenish our mess kit, and, perhaps, send letters to friends. We also desire to establish an astronomic station here; and hence this will be our stopping place for several days.

Some years ago, Captain Berthoud[5] surveyed a stage route from Salt Lake City to Denver, and this is the place where he crossed the Green River. His party was encamped here for some time, constructing a ferry boat and opening a road.

A little above the mouth of the Uinta, on the west side of the Green, there is a lake of several thousand acres.[6] We carry our boat across the divide between this and the river, have a row on its quiet waters, and succeed in shooting several ducks.

---

[5] Swiss immigrant and Civil War veteran, Edward Louis Berthoud (1828–1910). His route is followed today by U.S. Highway 40 (Davies, 1934). His survey party went through in 1861.
[6] The lake is probably that which is in Stewart Lake Waterfowl Management Area. What he calls the Uinta here is probably what is today named Ashley Creek. The Uinta is part of the Duchesne, which enters the Green father downstream.

June 29.—A mile and three quarters from here is the junction of the White River with the Green.[7] The White has its source far to the east, in the Rocky Mountains. This morning, I cross the Green, and go over into the valley of the White, and extend my walk several miles along its winding way, until, at last, I come in sight of some strangely carved rocks, named by General Hughes, in his journal, "Goblin City."[8] Our last winter's camp was situated a hundred miles above the point reached today. The course of the river, for much of the distance, is through cañons; but, at some places, valleys are found. Excepting these little valleys, the region is one of great desolation: arid, almost treeless, bluffs, hills, ledges of rock, and drifting sands. Along the course of the Green, however, from the foot of Split Mountain cañon to a point some distance below the mouth of the Uinta, there are many groves of cottonwood, natural meadows, and rich lands. This arable belt extends some distance up the White River, on the east, and the Uinta, on the west, and the time must soon come when settlers will penetrate this country, and make homes.

June 30.—We have a row up the Uinta[9] today, but are not able to make much headway against the swift current, and hence conclude we must walk all the way to the agency.

July 1.—Two days have been employed in obtaining the local time, taking observations for latitude and longitude, and making excursions into the adjacent country. This morning, with two of the men, I start for the Agency. It is a toilsome walk, twenty miles of the distance being across a sand desert. Occasionally, we have to wade the river, crossing it back and forth. Toward evening, we cross several beautiful streams, which are tributaries of the Uinta, and we pass through pine groves and meadows, arriving just at dusk at the

---

[7] This is south of the Ouray National Wildlife Refuge and north of the Pariette Wetlands. Powell must have written this from just above the mouth of the Duchesne River.

[8] This is not the same as today's Goblin Valley State Park, which also has bizarre rock formations. It's unlikely that he's referring to Fantasy Canyon, as that would have been an awfully long walk in one day. I was unable to find records of the earlier expedition or the identity of General Hughes.

[9] Again, what Powell is calling the Uinta is today the Duchesne.

Reservation. Captain Dodds,[10] the agent, is away, having gone to Salt Lake City, but his assistants received us very kindly. It is rather pleasant to see a house once more, and some evidences of civilization, even if it is on an Indian reservation, several days' ride from the nearest home of the white man.

July 2.—I go, this morning, to visit *Tsau'-wi-at*. This old chief is but the wreck of a man, and no longer has influence. Looking at him, you can scarcely realize that he is a man. His skin is shrunken, wrinkled, and dry, and seems to cover no more than a form of bones. He is said to be more than a hundred years old. I talk a little with him, but his conversation is incoherent, though he seems to take pride in showing me some medals, that must have been given him many years ago. He has a pipe which, he says, he has used a long time. I offer to exchange with him, and he seems to be glad to accept; so I add another to my collection of pipes. His wife, "The Bishop," as she is called, is a very garrulous old woman; she exerts a great influence, and is much revered. She is the only Indian woman I have known to occupy a place in the council ring. She seems very much younger than her husband, and, though wrinkled and ugly, is still vigorous. She has much to say to me concerning the condition of the people, and seems very anxious that they should learn to cultivate the soil, own farms, and live like white men. After talking a couple of hours with these old people, I go to see the farms. They are situated in a very beautiful district, where many fine streams of water meander across alluvial plains and meadows. These creeks have quite a fall, and it is very easy to take their waters out above, and, with them, overflow the lands.

It will be remembered that irrigation is necessary, in this dry climate, to successful farming. Quite a number of Indians have each a patch of ground, of two or three acres, on which they are raising wheat, potatoes, turnips, pumpkins, melons, and other vegetables. Most of the crops are looking well, and it is rather surprising with

[10] Pardon Dodds (1837-1921). The Uintah and Ouray Indian Reservation is home of the Ute Tribe. The agency in 1869, according to two sources, was on the Whiterocks River and later moved to Fort Duchesne, where the tribal council sits in the 21st century. Powell could easily have walked the twenty miles to Fort Duchesne in a long day.

what pride they show us that they are able to cultivate crops like white men. They are still occupying lodges, and refuse to build houses, assigning as a reason that when any one dies in a lodge it is always abandoned, and very often burned with all the effects of the deceased, and when houses have been built for them they have been treated in the same way. With their unclean habits, a fixed residence would doubtless be no pleasant place. This beautiful valley has been the home of a people of a higher grade of civilization than the present Utes. Evidences of this are quite abundant; on our way here yesterday we discovered, in many places along the trail, fragments of pottery; and wandering about the little farms today, I find the foundations of ancient houses, and mealing stones that were not used by nomadic people, as they are too heavy to be transported by such tribes, and are deeply worn. The Indians, seeing that I am interested in these matters, take pains to show me several other places where these evidences remain, and tell me that they know nothing about the people who formerly dwelt here. They further tell me that up in the cañon the rocks are covered with pictures.

July 5.—The last two days have been spent in studying the language of the Indians, and making collections of articles illustrating the state of arts among them.

Frank Goodman informs me this morning that he has concluded not to go on with the party, saying that he has seen danger enough. It will be remembered that he was one of the crew on the *No Name* when she was wrecked. As our boats are rather heavily loaded, I am content that he should leave, although he has been a faithful man.

We start early on our return to the boats, taking horses with us from the reservation, and two Indians, who are to bring the animals back.

Whirlpool cañon is fourteen and a quarter miles in length, the walls varying from one thousand eight hundred to two thousand four hundred feet in height. The course of the river through Island Park is nine miles. Split Mountain cañon is eight miles long. The highest crags on its walls reach an altitude above the river of from two thousand five hundred to two thousand seven hundred feet. In these cañons, cedars only are found on the walls.

The distance by river from the foot of Split Mountain cañon to the mouth of the Uinta is sixty-seven miles. The valley through which it runs is the home of many antelope, and we have adopted the Indian name, *Won'-sits Yu-av*—Antelope Valley.

THE JUNCTION OF THE GRAND AND GREEN

JULY 6.—Start early this morning. A short distance below the mouth of the Uinta, we come to the head of a long island. Last winter, a man named Johnson, a hunter and Indian trader, visited us at our camp in White River Valley. This man has an Indian wife, and, having no fixed home, usually travels with one of the Ute bands. He informed me it was his intention to plant some corn, potatoes, and other vegetables on this island in the spring, and, knowing that we would pass it, invited us to stop and help ourselves, even if he should not be there; so we land and go out on the island. Looking about, we soon discover his garden, but it is in a sad condition, having received no care since it was planted. It is yet too early in the season for corn, but Hall suggests that potato tops are good greens, and, anxious for some change from our salt meat fare, we gather a quantity and take them aboard. At noon we stop and cook our greens for dinner; but soon, one after another of the party is taken sick; nausea first, and then severe vomiting, and we tumble around under the trees, groaning with pain, and I feel a little alarmed, lest our poisoning be severe. Emetics are administered to those who are willing to take them, and about the middle of the afternoon we are all rid of the pain. Jack Sumner records in his diary that "Potato tops are not good greens on the sixth day of July."[1]

This evening we enter another cañon, almost imperceptibly, as the walls rise very gently.

July 7.—We find quiet water today, the river sweeping in great and beautiful curves, the cañon walls steadily increasing in altitude. The escarpment formed by the cut edges of the rock are often vertical, sometimes terraced, and in some places the treads of the terraces are sloping. In these quiet curves vast amphitheaters are formed, now in vertical rocks, now in steps.

The salient point of rock within the curve is usually broken down in a steep slope, and we stop occasionally to climb up, at such a place, where, on looking down, we can see the river sweeping the

---

[1] Potato tops do make good greens when they are young, but become poisonous as they mature, like poke shoots.—note in original by editor

51

foot of the opposite cliff, in a great, easy curve, with a perpendicular or terraced wall rising from the water's edge many hundreds of feet. One of these we find very symmetrical, and name it Sumner's Amphitheater. The cliffs are rarely broken by the entrance of side cañons, and we sweep around curve after curve, with almost continuous walls, for several miles.

Late in the afternoon, we find the river much rougher, and come upon rapids, not dangerous, but still demanding close attention.

We camp at night on the right bank, having made today twenty-six miles.

July 8.—This morning, Bradley and I go out to climb, and gain an altitude of more than two thousand feet above the river, but still do not reach the summit of the wall.

After dinner, we pass through a region of the wildest desolation. The cañon is very tortuous, the river very rapid, and many lateral cañons enter on either side. These usually have their branches, so that the region is cut into a wilderness of gray and brown cliffs. In several places, these lateral cañons are only separated from each other by narrow walls, often hundreds of feet high, but so narrow in places that where softer rocks are found below, they have crumbled away, and left holes in the wall, forming passages from one cañon into another. These we often call natural bridges; but they were never intended to span streams. They had better, perhaps, be called side doors between cañon chambers.

Piles of broken rock lie against these walls; crags and tower shaped peaks are seen everywhere; and away above them, long lines of broken cliffs, and above and beyond the cliffs are pine forests, of which we obtain occasional glimpses, as we look up through a vista of rocks.

The walls are almost without vegetation; a few dwarf bushes are seen here and there, clinging to the rocks, and cedars grow from the crevices—not like the cedars of a land refreshed with rains, great cones bedecked with spray, but ugly clumps, like war clubs, beset with spines. We are minded to call this the cañon of Desolation.

The wind annoys us much today. The water, rough by reason of the rapids, is made more so by head gales. Wherever a great face of rock has a southern exposure, the rarified air rises, and the wind rushes in below, either up or down the cañon, or both, causing local currents.

Just at sunset, we run a bad rapid, and camp at its foot.

July 9.—Our run today is through a cañon, with ragged, broken walls, many lateral gulches or cañons entering on either side. The river is rough, and occasionally it becomes necessary to use lines in passing rocky places. During the afternoon, we come to a rather open cañon valley, stretching up toward the west, its farther end lost in the mountains. From a point to which we climb, we obtain a good view of its course, until its angular walls are lost in the vista.

July 10.—Sumner, who is a fine mechanist, is learning to take observations for time with the sextant. Today, he remains in camp to practice.

Howland and myself determine to climb out, and start up a lateral cañon, taking a barometer with us, for the purpose of measuring the thickness of the strata over which we pass. The readings of a barometer below are recorded every half hour, and our observations must be simultaneous. Where the beds, which we desire to measure, are very thick, we must climb with the utmost speed, to reach their summits in time. Again, where there are thinner beds, we wait for the moment to arrive; and so, by hard and easy stages, we make our way to the top of the cañon wall, and reach the plateau above about two o'clock.

Howland, who has his gun with him, sees deer feeding a mile or two back, and goes off for a hunt. I go to a peak, which seems to be the highest one in this region, about half a mile distant, and climb, for the purpose of tracing the topography of the adjacent country. From this point, a fine view is obtained. A long plateau stretches across the river, in an easterly and westerly direction, the summit covered by pine forests, with intervening elevated valleys and gulches. The plateau itself is cut in two by the cañon. Other side cañons head away back from the river, and run down into the Green.

Besides these, deep and abrupt cañons are seen to head back on the plateau, and run north toward the Uinta and White Rivers. Still other cañons head in the valleys, and run toward the south. The elevation of the plateau being about eight thousand feet above the level of the sea, brings it into a region of moisture, as is well attested by the forests and grassy valleys. The plateau seems to rise gradually to the west, until it merges into the Wasatch Mountains. On these high table lands, elk and deer abound; and they are favorite hunting grounds for the Ute Indians.

A little before sunset, Howland and I meet again at the head of the side cañon, and down we start. It is late, and we must make great haste, or be caught by the darkness; so we go, running where we can; leaping over the ledges; letting each other down on the loose rocks, as long as we can see.

When darkness comes, we are still some distance from camp, and a long, slow, anxious descent we make, towards the gleaming camp fire.

After supper, observations for latitude are taken, and only two or three hours for sleep remain, before daylight.

July 11.—A short distance below camp we run a rapid, and, in doing so, break an oar, and then lose another, both belonging to the *Emma Dean*. So the pioneer boat has but two oars.

We see nothing of which oars can be made, so we conclude to run on to some point, where it seems possible to climb out to the forests on the plateau, and there we will procure suitable timber from which to make new ones.

We soon approach another rapid. Standing on deck, I think it can be run, and on we go. Coming nearer, I see that at the foot it has a short turn to the left, where the waters pile up against the cliff. Here we try to land, but quickly discover that, being in swift water, above the fall, we cannot reach shore, crippled, as we are, by the loss of two oars; so the bow of the boat is turned down stream. We shoot by a big rock; a reflex wave rolls over our little boat and fills her. I see the place is dangerous, and quickly signal to the other boats to land where they can. This is scarcely completed when another wave rolls our boat over, and I am thrown some distance into the water. I soon find that swimming is very easy, and I cannot sink.[2] It is only necessary to ply strokes sufficient to keep my head out of the water, though now and then, when a breaker rolls over me, I close my mouth, and am carried through it. The boat is drifting ahead of me twenty or thirty feet, and, when the great waves are passed, I overtake it, and find Sumner and Dunn clinging to her. As soon as we reach quiet water, we all swim to one side and turn her over. In doing this, Dunn loses his hold and goes under; when he comes up, he is caught by Sumner and pulled to the boat. In the meantime we have drifted downstream some distance, and see another rapid below. How bad it may be we cannot tell, so we swim toward shore, pulling our boat with us, with all the vigor possible, but are carried down much faster than distance toward shore is gained. At last we reach a huge pile of driftwood. Our rolls of blankets, two guns, and a barometer were in the open compartment of the boat, and, when it went over, these were thrown out. The guns and barometer are lost, but I succeeded in catching one of the rolls of blankets, as it drifted by, when we were swimming to shore; the other two are lost, and sometimes hereafter we may sleep cold.

A huge fire is built on the bank, our clothing is spread to dry, and then from the drift logs we select one from which we think oars can be made, and the remainder of the day is spent in sawing them out.

July 12.—This morning, the new oars are finished, and we start once more. We pass several bad rapids, making a short portage at one, and before noon we come to a long, bad fall, where the channel is filled with rocks on the left, turning the waters to the right, where they pass under an overhanging rock. On examination, we determine to run it, keeping as close to the left hand rocks as safety will permit, in order to avoid the overhanging cliff. The little boat runs over all right; another follows, but the men are not able to keep her near enough to the left bank, and she is carried, by a swift chute, into great waves to the right, where she is tossed about, and Bradley is knocked over the side, but his foot catching under the seat, he is

---

[2] Powell was the only team member with a life preserver, a necessity for a one-armed man (USGS website).

dragged along in the water, with his head down; making great exertion, he seizes the gunwale with his left hand, and can lift his head above water now and then. To us who are below, it seems impossible to keep the boat from going under the overhanging cliff; but Powell, for the moment, heedless of Bradley's mishap, pulls with all his power for half a dozen strokes, when the danger is past; then he seizes Bradley, and pulls him in. The men in the boat above, seeing this, land, and she is let down by lines.

Just here we emerge from the cañon of Desolation, as we have named it, into a more open country, which extends for a distance of nearly a mile, when we enter another cañon, cut through gray sandstone.

About three o'clock in the afternoon we meet with a new difficulty. The river fills the entire channel; the walls are vertical on either side, from the water's edge, and a bad rapid is beset with rocks. We come to the head of it, and land on a rock in the stream; the little boat is let down to another rock below, the men of the larger boat holding to the line; the second boat is let down in the same way, and the line of the third boat is brought with them. Now, the third boat pushes out from the upper rock, and, as we have her line below, we pull in and catch her, as she is sweeping by at the foot of the rock on which we stand. Again the first boat is let downstream the full length of her line, and the second boat is passed down by the first to the extent of her line, which is held by the men in the first boat; so she is two lines' length from where she started. Then the third boat is let down past the second, and still down, nearly to the length of her line, so that she is fast to the second boat, and swinging down three lines' lengths, with the other two boats intervening. Held in this way, the men are able to pull her into a cove, in the left wall, where she is made fast. But this leaves a man on the rock above, holding to the line of the little boat. When all is ready, he springs from the rock, clinging to the line with one hand, and swimming with the other, and we pull him in as he goes by. As the two boats, thus loosened, drift down, the men in the cove pull us all in, as we come opposite; then we pass around to a point of rock below the cove, close to the wall, land, and make a short portage over the worst places in the rapid, and start again.

At night we camp on a sand beach; the wind blows a hurricane; the drifting sand almost blinds us; and nowhere can we find shelter. The wind continues to blow all night; the sand sifts through our blankets, and piles over us, until we are covered as in a snow-drift. We are glad when morning comes.

July 13.—This morning, we have an exhilarating ride. The river is swift, and there are many smooth rapids. I stand on deck, keeping careful watch ahead, and we glide along, mile after mile, plying strokes now on the right, and then on the left, just sufficient to guide our boats past the rocks into smooth water. At noon we emerge from Gray cañon,[3] as we have named it, and camp, for dinner, under a cottonwood tree, standing on the left bank.

Extensive sand plains extend back from the immediate river valley, as far as we can see, on either side. These naked, drifting sands gleam brilliantly in the midday sun of July. The reflected heat from the glaring surface produces a curious motion of the atmosphere; little currents are generated, and the whole seems to be trembling and moving about in many directions, or, failing to see that the movement is in the atmosphere, it gives the impression of an unstable land. Plains, and hills, and cliffs, and distant mountains seem vaguely to be floating about in a trembling, wave rocked sea, and patches of landscape will seem to float away, and be lost, and then re-appear.

Just opposite, there are buttes, that are outliers of cliffs to the left. Below, they are composed of shales and marls of light blue and slate colors; and above, the rocks are buff and gray, and then brown. The buttes are buttressed below, where the azure rocks are seen, and terraced above through the gray and brown beds. A long line of cliffs or rock escarpments separate the table lands, through which Gray cañon is cut, from the lower plain. The eye can trace these azure beds and cliffs, on either side of the river, in a long line, extending

---

[3] This is just over ten miles north by river above present-day Green River State Park.

57

across its course, until they fade away in the perspective. These cliffs are many miles in length, and hundreds of feet high; and all these buttes—great mountain-masses of rock—are dancing and fading away, and re-appearing, softly moving about, or so they seem to the eye, as seen through the shifting atmosphere.

This afternoon, our way is through a valley, with cottonwood groves on either side. The river is deep, broad, and quiet.

About two hours from noon camp, we discover an Indian crossing, where a number of rafts, rudely constructed of logs and bound together by withes, are floating against the bank. On landing, we see evidences that a party of Indians have crossed within a very few days. This is the place where the lamented Gunnison[4] crossed, in the year 1853, when making an exploration for a railroad route to the Pacific coast.

An hour later, we run a long rapid, and stop at its foot to examine some curious rocks, deposited by mineral springs that at one time must have existed here, but which are no longer flowing.

July 14.—This morning, we pass some curious black bluffs on the right, then two or three short cañons, and then we discover the mouth of the San Rafael,[5] a stream which comes down from the distant mountains in the west. Here we stop for an hour or two, and take a short walk up the valley, and find it is a frequent resort for Indians. Arrowheads are scattered about, many of them very beautiful. Flint chips are seen strewn over the ground in great profusion, and the trails are well worn.

Starting after dinner, we pass some beautiful buttes on the left, many of which are very symmetrical. They are chiefly composed of

----

[4] John Williams Gunnison (1812–1853), army officer and noted explorer. On the morning of October 26, 1853, Gunnison and the eleven men in his party were allegedly attacked by a band of Utes; he and seven of his men were killed. Investigation threw suspicion on Mormons for the attack (nps.gov website). A number of towns and geographical features bear Gunnison's name.

[5] This is very near the White Wash Sand Dunes Recreation Area on the opposite side of the Green River.

gypsum of many hues, from light gray to slate color; then pink, purple, and brown beds.

Now, we enter another cañon. Gradually the walls rise higher and higher as we proceed, and the summit of the cañon is formed of the same beds of orange colored sandstone. Back from the brink, the hollows of the plateau are filled with sand disintegrated from these orange beds. They are of rich cream color, shaded into maroon, everywhere destitute of vegetation, and drifted into long, wave like ridges.

The course of the river is tortuous, and it nearly doubles upon itself many times. The water is quiet, and constant rowing is necessary to make much headway. Sometimes, there is a narrow flood plain between the river and the wall, on one side or the other. Where these long, gentle curves are found, the river washes the very foot of the outer wall. A long peninsula of willow bordered meadow projects within the curve, and the talus, at the foot of the cliff, is usually covered with dwarf oaks. The orange colored sandstone is very homogeneous in structure, and the walls are usually vertical, though not very high. Where the river sweeps around a curve under a cliff, a vast hollow dome may be seen, with many caves and deep alcoves, that are greatly admired by the members of the party, as we go by.

We camp at night on the left bank.

July 15.—Our camp is in a great bend of the cañon. The perimeter of the curve is to the west, and we are on the east side of the river. Just opposite, a little stream comes down through a narrow side cañon. We cross, and go up to explore it. Just at its mouth, another lateral cañon enters, in the angle between the former and the main cañon above. Still another enters in the angle between the cañon below and the side cañon first mentioned, so that three side cañons enter at the same point. These cañons are very tortuous, almost closed in from view, and, seen from the opposite side of the river, they appear like three alcoves; and we name this Trin-Alcove Bend.[6]

---

[6] Still known by that name today; it's about 15 miles in a direct line from the boundary of Canyonlands National Park.

Going up the little stream, in the central cove, we pass between high walls of sandstone, and wind about in glens. Springs gush from the rocks at the foot of the walls; narrow passages in the rocks are threaded, caves are entered, and many side cañons are observed.

The right cove is a narrow, winding gorge, with overhanging walls, almost shutting out the light.

The left is an amphitheater, turning spirally up, with overhanging shelves. A series of basins, filled with water, are seen at different altitudes, as we pass up; huge rocks are piled below on the right, and overhead there is an arched ceiling. After exploring these alcoves, we recross the river, and climb the rounded rocks on the point of the bend. In every direction, as far as we are able to see, naked rocks appear. Buttes are scattered on the landscape, here rounded into cones, there buttressed, columned, and carved in quaint shapes, with deep alcoves and sunken recesses. All about us are basins, excavated in the soft sandstones; and these have been filled by the late rains.

Over the rounded rocks and water pockets we look off on a fine stretch of river, and beyond are naked rocks and beautiful buttes to the Azure Cliffs, and beyond these, and above them, the Brown Cliffs, and still beyond, mountain peaks; and clouds piled over all.

On we go, after dinner, with quiet water, still compelled to row, in order to make fair progress. The cañon is yet very tortuous.

About six miles below noon camp, we go around a great bend to the right, five miles in length, and come back to a point within a quarter of a mile of where we started. Then we sweep around another great bend to the left, making a circuit of nine miles, and come back to the point within six hundred yards of the beginning of the bend. In the two circuits, we describe almost the figure 8. The men call it a bow-knot of river; so we name it Bow-Knot Bend.[7] The line of the figure is fourteen miles in length.

---

[7] On maps today as Bowknot Bend. High walls separate the loops of the river here, preventing an easy portage over a short span.

There is an exquisite charm in our ride today down this beautiful cañon. It gradually grows deeper with every mile of travel; the walls are symmetrically curved, and grandly arched; of a beautiful color, and reflected in the quiet waters in many places, so as to almost deceive the eye, and suggest the thought, to the beholder, that he is looking into profound depths. We are all in fine spirits, feel very gay, and the badinage of the men is echoed from wall to wall. Now and then we whistle, or shout, or discharge a pistol, to listen to the reverberations among the cliffs.

At night we camp on the south side of the great Bow-Knot, and, as we eat our supper, which is spread on the beach, we name this Labyrinth cañon.

July 16.—Still we go down, on our winding way. We pass tower cliffs, then we find the river widens out for several miles, and meadows are seen on either side, between the river and the walls. We name this expansion of the river Tower Park.

At two o'clock we emerge from Labyrinth cañon, and go into camp.

July 17.—The line which separates Labyrinth cañon from the one below is but a line, and at once, this morning, we enter another cañon. The water fills the entire channel, so that nowhere is there room to land. The walls are low, but vertical, and, as we proceed, they gradually increase in altitude. Running a couple of miles, the river changes its course many degrees, toward the east. Just here, a little stream comes in on the right, and the wall is broken down; so we land, and go out to take a view of the surrounding country. We are now down among the buttes, and in a region the surface of which is naked, solid rock—a beautiful red sandstone, forming a smooth, undulating pavement. The Indians call this the "*Toom'-pin Tu-weap'*" or "Rock Land," and the "*Toom'-pin wu-near' Tu-weap'*" or "Land of Standing Rock."[8]

Off to the south we see a butte, in the form of a fallen cross. It is several miles away, still it presents no inconspicuous figure on the

---

[8] They were inside what is now Canyonlands National Park.

landscape, and must be many hundreds of feet high, probably more than two thousand. We note its position on our map, and name it "The Butte of the Cross."[9]

We continue our journey. In many places the walls, which rise from the water's edge, are overhanging on either side. The stream is still quiet, and we glide along, through a strange, weird, grand region. The landscape everywhere, away from the river, is of rock— cliffs of rock; tables of rock; plateaus of rock; terraces of rock; crags of rock—ten thousand strangely carved forms. Rocks everywhere, and no vegetation; no soil; no sand. In long, gentle curves, the river winds about these rocks.

When speaking of these rocks, we must not conceive of piles of boulders, or heaps of fragments, but a whole land of naked rock, with giant forms carved on it: cathedral shaped buttes, towering hundreds or thousands of feet; cliffs that cannot be scaled, and cañon walls that shrink the river into insignificance, with vast, hollow domes, and tall pinnacles, and shafts set on the verge overhead, and all highly colored—buff, gray, red, brown, and chocolate; never lichened; never moss-covered; but bare, and often polished.

We pass a place where two bends of the river come together, an intervening rock having been worn away, and a new channel formed across. The old channel ran in a great circle around to the right, by what was once a circular peninsula; then an island; then the water left the old channel entirely, and passed through the cut, and the old bed of the river is dry. So the great circular rock stands by itself, with precipitous walls all about it, and we find but one place where it can be scaled. Looking from its summit, a long stretch of river is seen, sweeping close to the overhanging cliffs on the right, but having a little meadow between it and the wall on the left. The curve is very gentle and regular. We name this Bonita Bend.[10]

And just here we climb out once more, to take another bearing on The Butte of the Cross. Reaching an eminence, from which we can

_____

[9] On 21st century maps as Buttes of The Cross South.
[10] Easily seen today on maps or Google Earth.

overlook the landscape, we are surprised to find that our butte, with its wonderful form, is indeed two buttes, one so standing in front of the other that, from our last point of view, it gave the appearance of a cross.

Again, a few miles below Bonita Bend, we go out a mile or two along the rocks, toward the Orange Cliffs, passing over terraces paved with jasper.

The cliffs are not far away, and we soon reach them, and wander in some deep, painted alcoves, which attracted our attention from the river; then we return to our boats.

Late in the afternoon, the water becomes swift, and our boats make great speed. An hour of this rapid running brings us to the junction of the Grand [Colorado] and Green, the foot of Stillwater cañon, as we have named it.

These streams unite in solemn depths, more than one thousand two hundred feet below the general surface of the country. The walls of the lower end of Stillwater cañon are very beautifully curved, as the river sweeps in its meandering course. The lower end of the cañon through which the Grand comes down, is also regular, but much more direct, and we look up this stream, and out into the country beyond, and obtain glimpses of snow clad peaks, the summits of a group of mountains known as the Sierra La Sal. Down the Colorado, the cañon walls are much broken.

We row around into the Grand, and camp on its northwest bank; and here we propose to stay several days, for the purpose of determining the latitude and longitude, and the altitude of the walls. Much of the night is spent in making observations with the sextant.

The distance from the mouth of the Uinta to the head of the cañon of Desolation is twenty and three-quarters miles. The cañon of Desolation is ninety-seven miles long; Gray cañon thirty-six. The course of the river through Gunnison's Valley is twenty-seven and a quarter miles; Labyrinth cañon, sixty-two and a half miles.

In the cañon of Desolation, the highest rocks immediately over the river are about two thousand four hundred feet. This is at Log Cabin

Cliff. The highest part of the terrace is near the brink of the Brown Cliffs. Climbing the immediate walls of the cañon, and passing back to the cañon terrace, and climbing that, we find the altitude, above the river, to be 3,300 feet. The lower end of Gray cañon is about 2,000 feet; the lower end of Labyrinth cañon, 1,300 feet.

Stillwater cañon is forty-two and three-quarters miles long; the highest walls, 1,300 feet.

JULY 18.—The day is spent in obtaining the time, and spreading our rations, which, we find, are badly injured. The flour has been wet and dried so many times that it is all musty, and full of hard lumps. We make a sieve of mosquito netting, and run our flour through it, losing more than two hundred pounds by the process. Our losses, by the wrecking of the *No Name*, and by various mishaps since, together with the amount thrown away today, leave us little more than two months' supplies, and, to make them last thus long, we must be fortunate enough to lose no more.

We drag our boats on shore, and turn them over to recalk and pitch them, and Sumner is engaged in repairing barometers. While we are here, for a day or two, resting, we propose to put everything in the best shape for a vigorous campaign.

July 19.—Bradley and I start this morning to climb the left wall below the junction. The way we have selected is up a gulch. Climbing for an hour over and among the rocks, we find ourselves in a vast amphitheater,[1] and our way cut off. We clamber around to the left for half an hour, until we find that we cannot go up in that direction. Then we try the rocks around to the right, and discover a narrow shelf, nearly half a mile long. In some places, this is so wide that we pass along with ease; in others, it is so narrow and sloping that we are compelled to lie down and crawl. We can look over the edge of the shelf, down eight hundred feet, and see the river rolling and plunging among the rocks. Looking up five hundred feet, to the brink of the cliff, it seems to blend with the sky. We continue along, until we come to a point where the wall is again broken down. Up we climb. On the right, there is a narrow, mural point of rocks, extending toward the river, two or three hundred feet high, and six or eight hundred feet long. We come back to where this sets in, and find it cut off from the main wall by a great crevice. Into this we pass. And now, a long, narrow rock is between us and the river. The rock itself is split longitudinally and transversely; and the rains on

---

[1] Powell may be describing the cliffs below what is now Confluence Overlook.

the surface above have run down through the crevices, and gathered into channels below, and then run off into the river. The crevices are usually narrow above, and, by erosion of the streams, wider below, forming a network of caves; but each cave having a narrow, winding sky-light up through the rocks.

We wander among these corridors for an hour or two, but find no place where the rocks are broken down, so that we can climb up. At last, we determine to attempt a passage by a crevice, and select one which we think is wide enough to admit of the passage of our bodies, and yet narrow enough to climb out by pressing our hands and feet against the walls. So we climb as men would out of a well. Bradley climbs first; I hand him the barometer, then climb over his head, and he hands me the barometer. So we pass each other alternately, until we emerge from the fissure, out on the summit of the rock. And what a world of grandeur is spread before us! Below is the cañon, through which the Colorado runs. We can trace its course for miles, and at points catch glimpses of the river. From the northwest comes the Green, in a narrow, winding gorge. From the northeast comes the Grand, through a cañon that seems bottomless from where we stand. Away to the west are lines of cliffs and ledges of rock—not such ledges as you may have seen where the quarryman splits his blocks, but ledges from which the gods might quarry mountains, that, rolled out on the plain below, would stand a lofty range; and not such cliffs as you may have seen where the swallow builds its nest, but cliffs where the soaring eagle is lost to view ere he reaches the summit.

Between us and the distant cliffs are the strangely carved and pinnacled rocks of the *Toom'-pin wu-near' Tu-weap*. On the summit of the opposite wall of the cañon are rock forms that we do not understand. Away to the east a group of eruptive mountains are seen—the Sierra La Sal. Their slopes are covered with pines, and deep gulches are flanked with great crags, and snow fields are seen near the summits. So the mountains are in uniform, green, gray, and silver. Wherever we look there is but a wilderness of rocks; deep gorges, where the rivers are lost below cliffs and towers and

66

pinnacles; and ten thousand strangely carved forms in every direction; and beyond them, mountains blending with the clouds.

Now we return to camp. While we are eating supper, we very naturally speak of better fare, as musty bread and spoiled bacon are not pleasant. Soon I see Hawkins down by the boat, taking up the sextant, rather a strange proceeding for him, and I question him concerning it. He replies that he is trying to find the latitude and longitude of the nearest pie.

July 20.—This morning, Captain Powell and I go out to climb the west wall of the cañon, for the purpose of examining the strange rocks seen yesterday from the other side. Two hours bring us to the top, at a point between the Green and Colorado, overlooking the junction of the rivers. A long neck of rock extends toward the mouth of the Grand. Out on this we walk, crossing a great number of deep crevices. Usually, the smooth rock slopes down to the fissure on either side. Sometimes it is an interesting question to us whether the slope is not so steep that we cannot stand on it. Sometimes, starting down, we are compelled to go on, and we are not always sure that the crevice is not too wide for a jump, when we measure it with our eye from above.

Probably the slopes would not be difficult if there was not a fissure at the lower end; nor would the fissures cause fear if they were but a few feet deep. It is curious how a little obstacle becomes a great obstruction, when a misstep would land a man in the bottom of a deep chasm. Climbing the face of a cliff, a man will walk along a step or shelf, but a few inches wide, without hesitancy, if the landing is but ten feet below, should he fall; but if the foot of the cliff is a thousand feet down, he will crawl. At last our way is cut off by a fissure so deep and wide that we cannot pass it. Then we turn and walk back into the country, over the smooth, naked sandstone, without vegetation, except that here and there dwarf cedars and pinon pines have found a footing in the huge cracks. There are great basins in the rock, holding water; some but a few gallons, others hundreds of barrels.

The day is spent in walking about through these strange scenes. A narrow gulch is cut into the wall of the main cañon. Follow this up, and you climb rapidly, as if going up a mountain side, for the gulch heads but a few hundred or a few thousand yards from the wall. But this gulch has its side gulches, and, as you come near to the summit, a group of radiating cañons is found. The spaces drained by these little cañons are terraced, and are, to a greater or less extent, of the form of amphitheaters, though some are oblong and some rather irregular. Usually, the spaces drained by any two of these little side cañons are separated by a narrow wall, one, two, or three hundred feet high, and often but a few feet in thickness. Sometimes the wall is broken into a line of pyramids above, and still remains a wall below. Now, there are a number of these gulches which break the wall of the main cañon of the Green, each one having its system of side cañons and amphitheaters, inclosed by walls, or lines of pinnacles.

The course of the Green, at this point, is approximately at right angles to that of the Colorado, and on the brink of the latter cañon we find the same system of terraced and walled glens. The walls, and pinnacles, and towers are of sandstone, homogeneous in structure, but not in color, as they show broad bands of red, buff, and gray. This painting of the rocks, dividing them into sections, increases their apparent height. In some places, these terraced and walled glens, along the Colorado, have coalesced with those along the Green; that is, the intervening walls are broken down. It is very rarely that a loose rock is seen. The sand is washed off so that the walls, terraces, and slopes of the glens are all of smooth sandstone.

In the walls themselves, curious caves and channels have been carved. In some places, there are little stairways up the walls; in others, the walls present what are known as royal arches; and so we wander through glens, and among pinnacles, and climb the walls from early morn until late in the afternoon.

July 21.—We start this morning on the Colorado. The river is rough, and bad rapids, in close succession, are found. Two very hard portages are made during the forenoon. After dinner, in running a rapid, the *Emma Dean* is swamped, and we are thrown into the river, we cling to her, and in the first quiet water below she is righted and bailed out; but three oars are lost in the mishap. The larger boats land above the dangerous place, and we make a portage, that occupies all the afternoon. We camp at night, on the rocks on the left bank, and can scarcely find room to lie down.

July 22.—This morning, we continue our journey, though short of oars. There is no timber growing on the walls within our reach, and no drift wood along the banks, so we are compelled to go on until something suitable can be found. A mile and three quarters below, we find a huge pile of drift wood, among which are some cottonwood logs. From these we select one which we think the best, and the men are set at work sawing oars. Our boats are leaking again, from the strains received in the bad rapids yesterday, so, after dinner, they are turned over, and some of the men are engaged in calking them.

Captain Powell and I go out to climb the wall to the east, for we can see dwarf pines above, and it is our purpose to collect the resin which oozes from them, to use in pitching our boats. We take a barometer with us, and find that the walls are becoming higher, for now they register an altitude, above the river, of nearly fifteen hundred feet.

July 23.—On starting, we come at once to difficult rapids and falls, that, in many places, are more abrupt than in any of the cañons through which we have passed, and we decide to name this Cataract cañon.

From morning until noon, the course of the river is to the west; the scenery is grand, with rapids and falls below, and walls above, beset with crags and pinnacles. Just at noon we wheel again to the south, and go into camp for dinner.[2]

While the cook is preparing it, Bradley, Captain Powell, and myself go up into a side cañon, that comes in at this point. We enter through a very narrow passage, having to wade along the course of a little stream until a cascade interrupts our progress. Then we climb to the right, for a hundred feet, until we reach a little shelf, along which we pass, walking with great care, for it is narrow, until we

---

[2] This is in the present area of Hite Overlook near Utah State Route 95.

pass around the fall. Here the gorge widens into a spacious, sky roofed chamber. In the farther end is a beautiful grove of cottonwoods, and between us and the cottonwoods the little stream widens out into three clear lakelets, with bottoms of smooth rock. Beyond the cottonwoods, the brook tumbles, in a series of white, shining cascades, from heights that seem immeasurable. Turning around, we can look through the cleft through which we came, and see the river, with towering walls beyond.

What a chamber for a resting place is this! hewn from the solid rock; the heavens for a ceiling; cascade fountains within; a grove in the conservatory, clear lakelets for a refreshing bath, and an outlook through the doorway on a raging river, with cliffs and mountains beyond.

Our way, after dinner, is through a gorge, grand beyond description. The walls are nearly vertical; the river broad and swift, but free from rocks and falls.[3] From the edge of the water to the brink of the cliffs it is one thousand six hundred to one thousand eight hundred feet. At this great depth, the river rolls in solemn majesty. The cliffs are reflected from the more quiet river, and we seem to be in the depths of the earth, and yet can look down into the waters that reflect a bottomless abyss. We arrive, early in the afternoon, at the head of more rapids and falls, but, wearied with past work, we determine to rest, so go into camp, and the afternoon and evening are spent by the men in discussing the probabilities of successfully navigating the river below. The barometric records are examined, to see what descent we have made since we left the mouth of the Grand, and what descent since we left the Pacific Railroad, and what fall there yet must be to the river, ere we reach the end of the great cañons. The conclusion to which the men arrive seems to be about this: that there are great descents yet to be made, but, if they are distributed in rapids and short falls, as they have been heretofore, we will be able to overcome them. But, may be, we shall come to a fall in these cañons which we cannot pass, where the walls rise from the water's edge, so that we cannot land, and where

---

[3] They had now entered an area which today contains waters backed up behind Glen Canyon Dam.

the water is so swift that we cannot return. Such places have been found, except that the falls were not so great but that we could run them with safety. How will it be in the future! So they speculate over the serious probabilities in jesting mood, and I hear Sumner remark, "My idea is, we had better go slow, and learn to peddle."

July 24.—We examine the rapids below. Large rocks have fallen from the walls—great, angular blocks, which have rolled down the talus, and are strewn along the channel. We are compelled to make three portages in succession, the distance being less than three-fourths of a mile, with a fall of seventy-five feet. Among these rocks, in chutes, whirlpools, and great waves, with rushing breakers and foam, the water finds its way, still tumbling down. We stop for the night, only three-fourths of a mile below the last camp. A very hard day's work has been done, and at evening I sit on a rock by the edge of the river, to look at the water, and listen to its roar. Hours ago, deep shadows had settled into the cañon as the sun passed behind the cliffs. Now, doubtless, the sun has gone down, for we can see no glint of light on the crags above. Darkness is coming on. The waves are rolling, with crests of foam so white they seem almost to give a light of their own. Nearby, a chute of water strikes the foot of a great block of limestone, fifty feet high, and the waters pile up against it, and roll back. Where there are sunken rocks, the water heaps up in mounds, or even in cones. At a point where rocks come very near the surface, the water forms a chute above, strikes, and is shot up ten or fifteen feet, and piles back in gentle curves, as in a fountain; and on the river tumbles and rolls.

July 25.—Still more rapids and falls today. In one, the *Emma Dean* is caught in a whirlpool, and set spinning about; and it is with great difficulty we are able to get out of it, with the loss of an oar. At noon, another is made; and on we go, running some of the rapids, letting down with lines past others, and making two short portages. We camp on the right bank, hungry and tired.[4]

---

[4] For modern readers, the left and right banks of rivers were oriented to looking downstream.

July 26.—We run a short distance this morning, and go into camp, to make oars and repair boats and barometers. The walls of the cañon have been steadily increasing in altitude to this point, and now they are more than two thousand feet high. In many places, they are vertical from the water's edge; in others, there is a talus between the river and the foot of the cliffs, and they are often broken down by side cañons. It is probable that the river is nearly as low now as it is ever found. High water mark can be observed forty, fifty, sixty, or a hundred feet above its present stage. Sometimes logs and drift wood are seen wedged into the crevice overhead, where floods have carried them.

About ten o'clock, Powell, Bradley, Howland, Hall, and myself start up a side cañon to the east. We soon come to pools of water; then to a brook, which is lost in the sands below; and, passing up the brook, we find the cañon narrows, the walls close in, are often overhanging, and at last we find ourselves in a vast amphitheater, with a pool of deep, clear, cold water on the bottom. At first, our way seems cut off; but we soon discover a little shelf, along which we climb, and, passing beyond the pool, walk a hundred yards or more, turn to the right, and find ourselves in another dome-shaped amphitheater. There is a winding cleft at the top, reaching out to the country above, nearly two thousand feet overhead. The rounded, basin shaped bottom is filled with water to the foot of the walls. There is no shelf by which we can pass around the foot. If we swim across, we meet with a face of rock hundreds of feet high, over which a little rill glides, and it will be impossible to climb. So we can go no further up this cañon. Then we turn back, and examine the walls on either side carefully, to discover, if possible, some way of climbing out.

In this search, every man takes his own course, and we are scattered. I almost abandon the idea of getting out, and am engaged in searching for fossils, when I discover, on the north, a broken place, up which it may be possible for me to climb. The way, for a distance, is up a slide of rocks; then up an irregular amphitheater, on points that form steps and give handhold, and then I reach a little shelf, along which I walk, and discover a vertical fissure, parallel to the face of the wall, and reaching to a higher shelf. This fissure is narrow, and I try to climb up to the bench, which is about forty feet overhead. I have a barometer on my back, which rather impedes my climbing. The walls of the fissure are of smooth limestone, offering neither foot nor hand hold. So I support myself by pressing my back against one wall and my knees against the other, and, in this way, lift my body, in a shuffling manner, a few inches at a time, until I have, perhaps, made twenty-five feet of the distance, when the crevice widens a little, and I cannot press my knees against the rocks in front with sufficient power to give me support in lifting my body, and I try to go back. This I cannot do without falling. So I struggle along sidewise, farther into the crevice, where it narrows. But by this time my muscles are exhausted, and I cannot climb longer; so I move still a little farther into the crevice, where it is so narrow and wedging that I can lie in it, and there I rest.

Five or ten minutes of this relief, and up once more I go, and reach the bench above. On this I can walk for a quarter of a mile, till I come to a place where the wall is again broken down, so that I can climb up still farther, and in an hour I reach the summit. I hang up my barometer, to give it a few minutes' time to settle, and occupy myself in collecting resin from the pinon pines, which are found in great abundance. One of the principal objects in making this climb was to get this resin, for the purpose of smearing our boats; but I have with me no means of carrying it down. The day is very hot, and my coat was left in camp, so I have no linings to tear out. Then it occurs to me to cut off the sleeve of my shirt, tie it up at one end, and in this little sack I collect about a gallon of pitch.

After taking observations for altitude, I wander back on the rock, for an hour or two, when suddenly I notice that a storm is coming from the south. I seek a shelter in the rocks; but when the storm bursts, it comes down as a flood from the heavens, not with gentle drops at first, slowly increasing in quantity, but as if suddenly poured out. I am thoroughly drenched, and almost washed away. It lasts not more than half an hour, when the clouds sweep by to the north, and I have sunshine again.

In the meantime, I have discovered a better way of getting down, and I start for camp, making the greatest haste possible. On reaching the bottom of the side cañon, I find a thousand streams rolling down, the cliffs on every side, carrying with them red sand; and these all unite in the cañon below, in one great stream of red mud.

Traveling as fast as I can run, I soon reach the foot of the stream, for the rain did not reach the lower end of the cañon, and the water is running down a dry bed of sand; and, although it comes in waves, several feet high and fifteen or twenty feet in width, the sands soak it up, and it is lost. But wave follows wave, and rolls along, and is swallowed up; and still the floods come on from above. I find that I can travel faster than the stream; so I hasten to camp, and tell the men there is a river coming down the cañon. We carry our camp equipage hastily from the bank, to where we think it will be above the water. Then we stand by, and see the river roll on to join the Colorado. Great quantities of gypsum are found at the bottom of the gorge; so we name it Gypsum cañon.

July 27.—We have more rapids and falls until noon; then we come to a narrow place in the cañon, with vertical walls for several hundred feet, above which are steep steps and sloping rocks back to the summits. The river is very narrow, and we make our way with great care and much anxiety, hugging the wall on the left, and carefully examining the way before us.

Late in the afternoon, we pass to the left, around a sharp point, which is somewhat broken down near the foot, and discover a flock of mountain sheep on the rocks, more than a hundred feet above us. We quickly land in a cove, out of sight, and away go all the hunters with their guns, for the sheep have not discovered us. Soon, we hear firing, and those of us who have remained in the boats climb up to see what success the hunters have had. One sheep has been killed, and two of the men are still pursuing them. In a few minutes, we hear firing again, and the next moment down come the flock, clattering over the rocks, within twenty yards of us. One of the hunters seizes his gun, and brings a second sheep down, and the next minute the remainder of the flock is lost behind the rocks. We all give chase; but it is impossible to follow their tracks over the naked rock, and we see them no more. Where they went out of this rock walled cañon is a mystery, for we can see no way of escape. Doubtless, if we could spare the time for the search, we could find some gulch up which they ran.

We lash our prizes to the deck of one of the boats, and go on for a short distance; but fresh meat is too tempting for us, and we stop early to have a feast. And a feast it is! Two fine, young sheep. We care not for bread, or beans, or dried apples tonight; coffee and mutton is all we ask.

July 28.—We make two portages this morning, one of them very long. During the afternoon we run a chute, more than half a mile in length, narrow and rapid. This chute has a floor of marble; the rocks dip in the direction in which we are going, and the fall of the stream conforms to the inclination of the beds; so we float on water that is gliding down an inclined plane. At the foot of the chute, the river turns sharply to the right, and the water rolls up against a rock which, from above, seems to stand directly athwart its course. As we approach it, we pull with all our power to the right, but it seems impossible to avoid being carried headlong against the cliff, and we are carried up high on the waves—not against the rocks, for the rebounding water strikes us, and we are beaten back, and pass on with safety, except that we get a good drenching.

After this, the walls suddenly close in, so that the cañon is narrower than we have ever known it. The water fills it from wall to wall, giving us no landing place at the foot of the cliff; the river is very swift, the cañon is very tortuous, so that we can see but a few hundred yards ahead; the walls tower over us, often overhanging so as to almost shut out the light. I stand on deck, watching with intense anxiety, lest this may lead us into some danger; but we glide along, with no obstruction, no falls, no rocks, and, in a mile and a half, emerge from the narrow gorge into a more open and broken portion of the cañon. Now that it is past, it seems a very simple thing indeed to run through such a place, but the fear of what might be ahead made a deep impression on us.

At three o'clock we arrive at the foot of Cataract cañon. Here a long cañon valley comes down from the east, and the river turns sharply to the west in a continuation of the line of the lateral valley. In the bend on the right, vast numbers of crags, and pinnacles, and tower shaped rocks are seen. We call it Mille Crag Bend.[5]

And now we wheel into another cañon, on swift water, unobstructed by rocks. This new cañon is very narrow and very straight, with walls vertical below and terraced above. The brink of the cliff is 1,300 feet above the water, where we enter it, but the rocks dip to the west, and, as the course of the cañon is in that direction, the walls are seen to slowly decrease in altitude. Floating down this narrow channel, and looking out through the cañon crevice away in the distance, the river is seen to turn again to the left, and beyond this point, away many miles, a great mountain is seen. Still floating down, we see other mountains, now to the right, now on the left, until a great mountain range is unfolded to view. We name this Narrow cañon, and it terminates at the bend of the river below.

As we go down to this point, we discover the mouth of a stream, which enters from the right. Into this our little boat is turned. One of the men in the boat following, seeing what we have done, shouts to Dunn, asking if it is a trout-stream. Dunn replies, much disgusted, that it is "a dirty devil," and by this name the river is to be known hereafter. The water is exceedingly muddy, and has an unpleasant odor.

Some of us go out for half a mile, and climb a butte to the north. The course of the Dirty Devil River[6] can be traced for many miles. It comes down through a very narrow cañon, and beyond it, to the southwest, there is a long line of cliffs, with a broad terrace, or bench, between it and the brink of the cañon, and beyond these cliffs

---

[5] Whether Powell or the 1915 editor got the manuscript out of order here is a mystery. However, they had already passed what is today labeled as Mille Crag Bend in Cataract Canyon on July 23rd.

[6] Powell afterwards renamed it Frémont River.—(Ed. 1915) This river empties into the Green at Hite Crossing and can still be seen on Google Earth to be quite muddy.—2020

is situated the range of mountains seen as we came down Narrow cañon.

Looking up the Colorado, the chasm through which it runs can be seen, but we cannot look down on its waters. The whole country is a region of naked rock, of many colors, with cliffs and buttes about us, and towering mountains in the distance.

July 29.—We enter a cañon today, with low, red walls. A short distance below its head we discover the ruins of an old building, on the left wall. There is a narrow plain between the river and the wall just here, and on the brink of a rock two hundred feet high stands this old house. Its walls are of stone, laid in mortar, with much regularity. It was probably built three stories high; the lower story is yet almost intact; the second is much broken down, and scarcely anything is left of the third. Great quantities of flint chips are found on the rocks nearby, and many arrow heads, some perfect, others broken; and fragments of pottery are strewn about in great profusion. On the face of the cliff, under the building, and along down the river, for two or three hundred yards, there are many etchings. Two hours are given to the examination of these interesting ruins, then we run down fifteen miles farther, and discover another group. The principal building was situated on the summit of the hill. A part of the walls are standing, to the height of eight or ten feet, and the mortar yet remains, in some places. The house was in the shape of an L, with five rooms on the ground floor, one in the angle, and two in each extension. In the space in the angle, there is a deep excavation. From what we know of the people in the province of Tusayan, who are, doubtless, of the same race as the former inhabitants of these ruins, we conclude that this was a "kiva," or underground chamber, in which their religious ceremonies were performed.

We leave these ruins, and run down two or three miles, and go into camp about midafternoon. And now I climb the wall and go out into the back country for a walk.

The sandstone, through which the cañon is cut, is red and homogeneous, being the same as that through which Labyrinth runs. The smooth, naked rock stretches out on either side of the river for many miles, but curiously carved mounds and cones are scattered everywhere, and deep holes are worn out. Many of these pockets are filled with water. In one of these holes, or wells, twenty feet deep, I find a tree growing. The excavation is so narrow that I can step from its brink to a limb on the tree, and descend to the bottom of the well down a growing ladder. Many of these pockets are pot-holes, being found in the courses of little rills, or brooks, that run during the rains which occasionally fall in this region; and often a few harder rocks, which evidently assisted in their excavation, can be found in their bottoms. Others, which are shallower, are not so easily explained. Perhaps they are found where softer spots existed in the sandstone, places that yielded more readily to atmospheric degradation, and where the loose sands were carried away by the winds.

Just before sundown, I attempt to climb a rounded eminence, from which I hope to obtain a good outlook on the surrounding country. It is formed of smooth mounds, piled one above another. Up these I climb, winding here and there, to find a practicable way, until near the summit they become too steep for me to proceed. I search about, a few minutes, for a more easy way, when I am surprised at finding a stairway, evidently cut in the rock by hands. At one place, where there is a vertical wall of ten or twelve feet, I find an old, rickety ladder. It may be that this was a watch-tower of that ancient people whose homes we have found in ruins. On many of the tributaries of the Colorado I have heretofore examined their deserted dwellings. Those that show evidences of being built during the latter part of their occupation of the country, are, usually, placed on the most inaccessible cliffs. Sometimes, the mouths of caves have been walled across, and there are many other evidences to show their anxiety to secure defensible positions. Probably the nomadic tribes were sweeping down upon them, and they resorted to these cliffs and cañons for safety. It is not unreasonable to suppose that this orange mound was used as a watch-tower. Here I stand, where these now lost people stood centuries ago, and look over this strange country. I gaze off to great mountains, in the northwest, which are slowly covered by the night until they are lost, and then I return to camp. It is no easy task to find my way down the wall in the darkness, and I clamber about until it is nearly midnight, before I arrive.

July 30.—We make good progress today, as the water, though smooth, is swift. Sometimes, the cañon walls are vertical to the top; sometimes, they are vertical below, and have a mound covered slope above; in other places, the slope, with its mounds, comes down to the water's edge.

Still proceeding on our way, we find the orange sandstone is cut in two by a group of firm, calcareous strata, and the lower bed is underlaid by soft gypsiferous shales. Sometimes, the upper homogeneous bed is a smooth, vertical wall, but usually it is carved with mounds, with gently meandering valley lines. The lower bed, yielding to gravity, as the softer shales below work out into the river, breaks into angular surfaces, often having a columnar appearance. One could almost imagine that the walls had been carved with a purpose, to represent giant architectural forms.

In the deep recesses of the walls, we find springs, with mosses and ferns on the moistened sandstone.

July 31.—We have a cool, pleasant ride today, through this part of the cañon. The walls are steadily increasing in altitude, the curves are gentle, and often the river sweeps by an arc of vertical wall, smooth and unbroken, and then by a curve that is variegated by royal arches, mossy alcoves, deep, beautiful glens, and painted grottos.

Soon after dinner, we discover the mouth of the San Juan,[7] where we camp. The remainder of the afternoon is given to hunting some way by which we can climb out of the cañon; but it ends in failure.

August 1.—We drop down two miles this morning, and go into camp again. There is a low, willow covered strip of land along the walls on the east. Across this we walk, to explore an alcove which we see from the river. On entering, we find a little grove of box-elder

[7] They were now in within what is today the Glen Canyon Recreational Area, where Lake Powell obscures much of what Powell's team saw. Across from the mouth of the San Juan, which enters on the east, is beautiful Reflection Canyon.

and cottonwood trees; and, turning to the right, we find ourselves in a vast chamber, carved out of the rock. At the upper end there is a clear, deep pool of water, bordered with verdure. Standing by the side of this, we can see the grove at the entrance. The chamber is more than two hundred feet high, five hundred feet long, and two hundred feet wide. Through the ceiling, and on through the rocks for a thousand feet above, there is a narrow, winding skylight; and this is all carved out by a little stream, which only runs during the few showers that fall now and then in this arid country. The waters from the bare rocks back of the cañon, gathering rapidly into a small channel, have eroded a deep side cañon, through which they run, until they fall into the farther end of this chamber. The rock at the ceiling is hard, the rock below, very soft and friable; and, having cut through the upper harder portion down into the lower and softer, the stream has washed out these friable sandstones; and thus the chamber has been excavated.

Here we bring our camp. When "Old Shady" sings us a song at night, we are pleased to find that this hollow in the rock is filled with sweet sounds. It was doubtless made for an academy of music by its storm born architects; so we name it Music Temple.

August 2.—We still keep our camp in Music Temple today.

I wish to obtain a view of the adjacent country, if possible; so, early in the morning, the men take me across the river, and I pass along by the foot of the cliff half a mile up stream, and then climb first up broken ledges, then two or three hundred yards up a smooth, sloping rock, and then pass out on a narrow ridge. Still, I find I have not attained an altitude from which I can overlook the region outside of the cañon; and so I descend into a little gulch, and climb again to a higher ridge, all the way along naked sandstone, and at last I reach a point of commanding view. I can look several miles up the San Juan, and a long distance up the Colorado; and away to the northwest I can see the Henry Mountains; to the northeast, the Sierra La Sal; to the southeast, unknown mountains; and to the southwest, the meandering of the cañon. Then I return to the bank of the river.

We sleep again in Music Temple.

August 3.—Start early this morning. The features of this cañon are greatly diversified. Still vertical walls at times. These are usually found to stand above great curves. The river, sweeping around these bends, undermines the cliffs in places. Sometimes, the rocks are overhanging; in other curves, curious, narrow glens are found. Through these we climb, by a rough stairway, perhaps several hundred feet, to where a spring bursts out from under an overhanging cliff, and where cottonwoods and willows stand, while, along the curves of the brooklet, oaks grow, and other rich vegetation is seen, in marked contrast to the general appearance of naked rock. We call these Oak Glens.

Other wonderful features are the many side cañons or gorges that we pass. Sometimes, we stop to explore these for a short distance. In some places, their walls are much nearer each other above than below, so that they look somewhat like caves or chambers in the rocks. Usually, in going up such a gorge, we find beautiful vegetation; but our way is often cut off by deep basins, or pot-holes, as they are called.

On the walls, and back many miles into the country, numbers of monument shaped buttes are observed. So we have a curious ensemble of wonderful features—carved walls, royal arches, glens, alcove gulches, mounds, and monuments. From which of these features shall we select a name? We decide to call it Glen cañon.[8]

Past these towering monuments, past these mounded billows of orange sandstone, past these oak set glens, past these fern decked alcoves, past these mural curves, we glide hour after hour, stopping now and then, as our attention is arrested by some new wonder, until we reach a point which is historic.

In the year 1776, Father Escalante, a Spanish priest, made an expedition from Santa Fe to the northwest, crossing the Grand and Green, and then passing down along the Wasatch Mountains and the southern plateaus, until he reached the Rio Virgin. His intention was to cross to the Mission of Monterey; but, from information

---

[8] In 1963, the Glen Canyon dam was completed, creating massive Lake Powell and submerging countless unique and beautiful features.

received from the Indians, he decided that the route was impracticable. Not wishing to return to Santa Fe over the circuitous route by which he had just traveled, he attempted to go by one more direct, and which led him across the Colorado, at a point known as El vado de los Padres.[9] From the description which we have read, we are enabled to determine the place. A little stream comes down through a very narrow side cañon from the west. It was down this that he came, and our boats are lying at the point where the ford crosses. A well beaten Indian trail is seen here yet. Between the cliff and the river there is a little meadow. The ashes of many camp fires are seen, and the bones of numbers of cattle are bleaching on the grass. For several years the Navajos have raided on the Mormons that dwell in the valleys to the west, and they doubtless cross frequently at this ford with their stolen cattle.

August 4.—Today the walls grow higher, and the cañon much narrower. Monuments are still seen on either side; beautiful glens, and alcoves, and gorges, and side cañons are yet found. After dinner, we find the river making a sudden turn to the northwest, and the whole character of the cañon changed. The walls are many hundreds of feet higher, and the rocks are chiefly variegated shales of beautiful colors—creamy orange above, then bright vermilion, and below, purple and chocolate beds, with green and yellow sands. We run four miles through this, in a direction a little to the west of north; wheel again to the west, and pass into a portion of the cañon where the characteristics are more like those above the bend. At night we stop at the mouth of a creek coming in from the right, and suppose it to be the Paria,[10] which was described to me last year by a Mormon missionary.

Here the cañon terminates abruptly in a line of cliffs, which stretches from either side across the river.

August 5.—With some feeling of anxiety, we enter a new cañon this morning. We have learned to closely observe the texture of the

---

9 The Ford of the Fathers.
10 If Powell was correct, they were now below the present location of Glen Canyon Dam and into present-day Arizona, traveling through Marble Canyon.

rock. In softer strata, we have a quiet river; in harder, we find rapids and falls. Below us are the limestones and hard sandstones, which we found in Cataract cañon. This bodes toil and danger. Besides the texture of the rocks, there is another condition which affects the character of the channel, as we have found by experience. Where the strata are horizontal, the river is often quiet; but, even though it may be very swift in places, no great obstacles are found. Where the rocks incline in the direction traveled, the river usually sweeps with great velocity, but still we have few rapids and falls. But where the rocks dip up stream, and the river cuts obliquely across the upturned formations, harder strata above, and softer below, we have rapids and falls. Into hard rocks, and into rocks dipping up stream, we pass this morning, and start on a long, rocky, mad rapid. On the left there is a vertical rock, and down by this cliff and around to the left we glide, just tossed enough by the waves to appreciate the rate at which we are traveling.

The cañon is narrow, with vertical walls, which gradually grow higher. More rapids and falls are found. We come to one with a drop of sixteen feet, around which we make a portage, and then stop for dinner.

Then a run of two miles, and another portage, long and difficult; then we camp for the night, on a bank of sand.

August 6.—Cañon walls, still higher and higher, as we go down through strata. There is a steep talus at the foot of the cliff, and, in some places, the upper parts of the walls are terraced.

About ten o'clock we come to a place where the river occupies the entire channel, and the walls are vertical from the water's edge. We see a fall below, and row up against the cliff. There is a little shelf, or rather a horizontal crevice, a few feet over our heads. One man stands on the deck of the boat, another climbs on his shoulders, and then into the crevice. Then we pass him a line, and two or three others, with myself, follow; then we pass along the crevice until it becomes a shelf, as the upper part, or roof, is broken off. On this we walk for a short distance, slowly climbing all the way, until we reach a point where the shelf is broken off, and we can pass no farther. Then we go back to the boat, cross the stream, and get some logs that have lodged in the rocks, bring them to our side, pass them along the crevice and shelf, and bridge over the broken place. Then we go on to a point over the falls, but do not obtain a satisfactory view. Then we climb out to the top of the wall, and walk along to find a point below the fall, from which it can be seen. From this point it seems possible to let down our boats, with lines, to the head of the rapids, and then make a portage; so we return, row down by the side of the cliff, as far as we dare, and fasten one of the boats to a rock. Then we let down another boat to the end of its line beyond the first, and the third boat to the end of its line below the second, which brings it to the head of the fall, and under an overhanging rock. Then the upper boat, in obedience to a signal, lets go; we pull in the line, and catch the nearest boat as it comes, and then the last. Then we make a portage, and go on.

We go into camp early this afternoon, at a place where it seems possible to climb out, and the evening is spent in "making observations for time."

August 7.—The almanac tells us that we are to have an eclipse of the sun today, so Captain Powell and myself start early, taking our instruments with us, for the purpose of making observations on the eclipse, to determine our longitude. Arriving at the summit, after four hours' hard climbing, to attain 2,300 feet in height, we hurriedly build a platform of rocks, on which to place our instruments, and quietly wait for the eclipse; but clouds come on, and rain falls, and sun and moon are obscured.

Much disappointed, we start on our return to camp, but it is late, and the clouds make the night very dark. Still we feel our way down among the rocks with great care, for two or three hours, though making slow progress indeed. At last we lose our way, and dare proceed no farther. The rain comes down in torrents, and we can find no shelter. We can neither climb up nor go down, and in the darkness dare not move about, but sit and "weather out" the night.

August 8.—Daylight comes, after a long, oh! how long a night, and we soon reach camp.

After breakfast we start again, and make two portages during the forenoon.

The limestone of this cañon is often polished, and makes a beautiful marble. Sometimes the rocks are of many colors—white, gray, pink, and purple, with saffron tints.

It is with very great labor that we make progress, meeting with many obstructions, running rapids, letting down our boats with lines, from rock to rock, and sometimes carrying boats and cargoes around bad places. We camp at night, just after a hard portage, under an overhanging wall, glad to find shelter from the rain. We have to search for some time to find a few sticks of driftwood, just sufficient to boil a cup of coffee.

The water sweeps rapidly in this elbow of river, and has cut its way under the rock, excavating a vast half circular chamber, which, if utilized for a theater, would give sitting to fifty thousand people. Objections might be raised against it, from the fact that, at high water, the floor is covered with a raging flood.

August 9.—And now, the scenery is on a grand scale. The walls of the cañon, 2,500 feet high, are of marble, of many beautiful colors, and often polished below by the waves, or far up the sides, where showers have washed the sands over the cliffs.

At one place I have a walk, for more than a mile, on a marble pavement, all polished and fretted with strange devices, and embossed in a thousand fantastic patterns. Through a cleft in the wall the sun shines on this pavement, which gleams in iridescent beauty.

I pass up into the cleft. It is very narrow, with a succession of pools standing at higher levels as I go back. The water in these pools is clear and cool, coming down from springs. Then I return to the pavement, which is but a terrace or bench, over which the river runs at its flood, but left bare at present. Along the pavement, in many places, are basins of clear water, in strange contrast to the red mud of the river. At length I come to the end of this marble terrace, and take again to the boat.

Riding down a short distance, a beautiful view is presented. The river turns sharply to the east, and seems inclosed by a wall, set with a million brilliant gems. What can it mean? Every eye is engaged, every one wonders. On coming nearer, we find fountains bursting from the rock, high overhead, and the spray in the sunshine forms the gems which bedeck the wall. The rocks below the fountain are covered with mosses, and ferns, and many beautiful flowering plants. We name it Vasey's Paradise, in honor of the botanist who traveled with us last year.[11]

We pass many side cañons today, that are dark, gloomy passages, back into the heart of the rocks that form the plateau through which this cañon is cut.

It rains again this afternoon. Scarcely do the first drops fall, when little rills run down the walls. As the storm comes on, the little rills increase in size, until great streams are formed. Although the walls of the cañon are chiefly limestone, the adjacent country is of red sandstone; and now the waters, loaded with these sands, come down in rivers of bright red mud, leaping over the walls in innumerable cascades. It is plain now how these walls are polished in many; places.

At last, the storm ceases, and we go on. We have cut through the sandstones and limestones met in the upper part of the cañon, and through one great bed of marble a thousand feet in thickness. In this, great numbers of caves are hollowed out, and carvings are seen, which suggest architectural forms, though on a scale so grand that architectural terms belittle them. As this great bed forms a distinctive feature of the cañon, we call it Marble cañon.

It is a peculiar feature of these walls, that many projections are set out into the river, as if the wall was buttressed for support. The walls themselves are half a mile high, and these buttresses are on a corresponding scale, jutting into the river scores of feet. In the recesses between these projections there are quiet bays, except at the foot of a rapid, when they are dancing eddies or whirlpools. Sometimes these alcoves have caves at the back, giving them the

---

[11] Botanist George S. Vasey (1822–1893).

appearance of great depth. Then other caves are seen above, forming vast, dome shaped chambers. The walls, and buttresses, and chambers are all of marble.

The river is now quiet; the cañon wider. Above, when the river is at its flood, the waters gorge up, so that the difference between high and low water mark is often fifty or even seventy feet; but here, high-water mark is not more than twenty feet above the present stage of the river. Sometimes there is a narrow flood plain between the water and the wall.

Here we first discover mesquite shrubs, or small trees, with finely divided leaves and pods, somewhat like the locust.

August 10.—Walls still higher; water, swift again. We pass several broad, ragged cañons on our right, and up through these we catch glimpses of a forest clad plateau, miles away to the west.

At two o'clock, we reach the mouth of the Colorado Chiquito.[12] This stream enters through a cañon, on a scale quite as grand as that of the Colorado itself. It is a very small river, and exceedingly muddy and salt. I walk up the stream three or four miles, this afternoon, crossing and recrossing where I can easily wade it. Then I climb several hundred feet at one place, and can see up the chasm, through which the river runs, for several miles. On my way back, I kill two rattlesnakes, and find, on my arrival, that another has been killed just at camp.

August 11.—We remain at this point today for the purpose of determining the latitude and longitude, measuring the height of the walls, drying our rations, and repairing our boats.

Captain Powell, early in the morning, takes a barometer, and goes out to climb a point between the two rivers.

I walk down the gorge to the left at the foot of the cliff, climb to a bench, and discover a trail, deeply worn in the rock. Where it crosses the side gulches, in some places, steps have been cut. I can see no evidence of its having been traveled for a long time. It was doubtless a path used by the people who inhabited this country anterior to the

---

[12] The Little Colorado River.

present Indian races—the people who built the communal houses, of which mention has been made.

I return to camp about three o'clock, and find that some of the men have discovered ruins, and many fragments of pottery; also, etchings and hieroglyphics on the rocks.

We find, tonight, on comparing the readings of the barometers, that the walls are about three thousand feet high—more than half a mile—an altitude difficult to appreciate from a mere statement of feet. The ascent is made, not by a slope such as is usually found in climbing a mountain, but is much more abrupt—often vertical for many hundreds of feet—so that the impression is that we are at great depths; and we look up to see but a little patch of sky.

Between the two streams, above the Colorado Chiquito, in some places the rocks are broken and shelving for six or seven hundred feet; then there is a sloping terrace, which can only be climbed by finding some way up a gulch; then, another terrace, and back, still another cliff. The summit of the cliff is three thousand feet above the river, as our barometers attest.

Our camp is below the Colorado Chiquito, and on the eastern side of the cañon.

August 12.—The rocks above camp are rust colored sandstones and conglomerates. Some are very hard; others quite soft. These all lie nearly horizontal, and the beds of softer material have been washed out, and left the harder, thus forming a series of shelves. Long lines of these are seen, of varying thickness, from one or two to twenty or thirty feet, and the spaces between have the same variability. This morning, I spend two or three hours in climbing among these shelves, and then I pass above them, and go up a long slope, to the foot of the cliff, and try to discover some way by which I can reach the top of the wall; but I find my progress cut off by an amphitheater. Then, I wander away around to the left, up a little gulch, and along benches, and climb, from time to time, until I reach an altitude of nearly two thousand feet, and can get no higher. From this point, I can look off to the west, up side cañons of the Colorado, and see the edge of a great plateau, from which streams run down into the Colorado, and deep gulches, in the escarpment which faces us, continued by cañons, ragged and flaring, and set with cliffs and towering crags, down to the river. I can see far up Marble cañon, to long lines of chocolate colored cliffs, and above these, the Vermilion Cliffs. I can see, also, up the Colorado Chiquito, through a very ragged and broken cañon, with sharp salients set out from the walls on either side, their points overlapping, so that a huge tooth of marble, on one side, seems to be set between two teeth on the opposite; and I can also get glimpses of walls, standing away back from the river, while over my head are mural escarpments, not possible to be scaled.

Cataract cañon is forty-one miles long. The walls are 1,300 feet high at its head, and they gradually increase in altitude to a point about half-way down, where they are 2,700 feet, and then decrease to 1,300 feet at the foot. Narrow cañon is nine and a half miles long, with walls 1,300 feet in height at the head, and coming down to the water at the foot.

There is very little vegetation in this cañon, or in the adjacent country. Just at the junction of the Grand and Green, there are a number of hackberry trees; and along the entire length of Cataract cañon, the high-water line is marked by scattered trees of the same species. A few nut-pines and cedars are found, and occasionally a red-bud or judas tree; but the general aspect of the cañons, and of the adjacent country, is that of naked rock.

The distance through Glen cañon is 149 miles. Its walls vary from two or three hundred to sixteen hundred feet. Marble cañon is 65-1/2 miles long. At its head, it is 200 feet deep, and steadily increases in depth to its foot, where its walls are 3,500 feet high.

AUGUST 13.—We are now ready to start on our way down the Great Unknown. Our boats, tied to a common stake, are chafing each other, as they are tossed by the fretful river. They ride high and buoyant, for their loads are lighter than we could desire. We have but a month's rations remaining. The flour has been resifted through the mosquito net sieve; the spoiled bacon has been dried, and the worst of it boiled; the few pounds of dried apples have been spread in the sun, and reshrunken to their normal bulk; the sugar has all melted, and gone on its way down the river; but we have a large sack of coffee. The lighting of the boats has this advantage: they will ride the waves better, and we shall have but little to carry when we make a portage.[1]

We are three-quarters of a mile in the depths of the earth, and the great river shrinks into insignificance, as it dashes its angry waves against the walls and cliffs, that rise to the world above; they are but puny ripples, and we but pigmies, running up and down the sands, or lost among the boulders.

We have an unknown distance yet to run; an unknown river yet to explore. What falls there are, we know not; what rocks beset the channel, we know not; what walls rise over the river, we know not. Ah, well! we may conjecture many things. The men talk as cheerfully as ever; jests are bandied about freely this morning; but to me the cheer is somber and the jests are ghastly.

With some eagerness, and some anxiety, and some misgiving, we enter the cañon below, and are carried along by the swift water through walls which rise from its very edge. They have the same structure as we noticed yesterday—tiers of irregular shelves below, and, above these, steep slopes to the foot of marble cliffs. We run six miles in a little more than half an hour, and emerge into a more open portion of the cañon, where high hills and ledges of rock intervene between the river and the distant walls. Just at the head of

---

[1] By August 17 the food supply was nearly at an end. The crew had to throw away the last of the spoiled bacon. They had a few dried apples and enough flour to make biscuits for only 10 more days (USGS website).

this open place the river runs across a dike; that is, a fissure in the rocks, open to depths below, has been filled with eruptive matter, and this, on cooling, was harder than the rocks through which the crevice was made, and, when these were washed away, the harder volcanic matter remained as a wall, and the river has cut a gate-way through it several hundred feet high, and as many wide. As it crosses the wall, there is a fall below, and a bad rapid, filled with boulders of trap; so we stop to make a portage. Then on we go, gliding by hills and ledges, with distant walls in view; sweeping past sharp angles of rock; stopping at a few points to examine rapids, which we find can be run, until we have made another five miles, when we land for dinner.[2]

Then we let down with lines, over a long rapid, and start again. Once more the walls close in, and we find ourselves in a narrow gorge, the water again filling the channel, and very swift. With great care, and constant watchfulness, we proceed, making about four miles this afternoon, and camp in a cave.

August 14.—At daybreak we walk down the bank of the river, on a little sandy beach, to take a view of a new feature in the cañon. Heretofore, hard rocks have given us bad river; soft rocks, smooth water; and a series of rocks harder than any we have experienced sets in. The river enters the granite!

We can see but a little way into the granite gorge, but it looks threatening.

After breakfast we enter on the waves. At the very introduction, it inspires awe. The cañon is narrower than we have ever before seen it; the water is swifter; there are but few broken rocks in the channel; but the walls are set, on either side, with pinnacles and crags; and sharp, angular buttresses, bristling with wind and wave polished spires, extend far out into the river.

Ledges of rocks jut into the stream, their tops sometimes just below the surface, sometimes rising few or many feet above; and

---

[2] Eleven miles from the mouth of the Little Colorado would have put them at the mouth of Unkar Creek for dinner. The final four miles that afternoon should have put them at the mouth of Red Canyon.

island ledges, and island pinnacles, and island towers break the swift course of the stream into chutes, and eddies, and whirlpools. We soon reach a place where a creek comes in from the left,[3] and just below, the channel is choked with boulders, which have washed down this lateral cañon and formed a dam, over which there is a fall of thirty or forty feet; but on the boulders we can get foothold, and we make a portage.

Three more such dams are found. Over one we make a portage; at the other two we find chutes, through which we can run.

As we proceed, the granite rises higher, until nearly a thousand feet of the lower part of the walls are composed of this rock.

About eleven o'clock we hear a great roar ahead, and approach it very cautiously. The sound grows louder and louder as we run, and at last we find ourselves above a long, broken fall, with ledges and pinnacles of rock obstructing the river. There is a descent of, perhaps, seventy-five or eighty feet in a third of a mile, and the rushing waters break into great waves on the rocks, and lash themselves into a mad, white foam.[4] We can land just above, but there is no foot-hold on either side by which we can make a portage. It is nearly a thousand feet to the top of the granite, so it will be impossible to carry our boats around, though we can climb to the summit up a side gulch, and, passing along a mile or two, can descend to the river. This we find on examination; but such a portage would be impracticable for us, and we must run the rapid, or abandon the river. There is no hesitation. We step into our boats, push off and away we go, first on smooth but swift water, then we strike a glassy wave, and ride to its top, down again into the trough, up again on a higher wave, and down and up on waves higher and still higher, until we strike one just as it curls back, and a breaker rolls over our little boat. Still, on we speed, shooting past projecting rocks, till the little boat is caught in a whirlpool, and spun around several times. At last we pull out again into the stream, and now the other boats have passed us. The open compartment of the *Emma*

---

[3] Probably Hance Creek.
[4] Probably Grapevine Rapids.

Dean is filled with water, and every breaker rolls over us. Hurled back from a rock, now on this side, now on that, we are carried into an eddy, in which we struggle for a few minutes, and are then out again, the breakers still rolling over us. Our boat is unmanageable, but she cannot sink, and we drift down another hundred yards, through breakers; how, we scarcely know. We find the other boats have turned into an eddy at the foot of the fall, and are waiting to catch us as we come, for the men have seen that our boat is swamped. They push out as we come near, and pull us in against the wall. We bail our boat, and on we go again.

The walls, now, are more than a mile in height—a vertical distance difficult to appreciate. Stand on the south steps of the Treasury building in Washington, and look down Pennsylvania Avenue to the Capitol Park, and measure this distance overhead, and imagine cliffs to extend to that altitude, and you will understand what I mean; or, stand at Canal Street, in New York, and look up Broadway to Grace Church, and you have about the distance; or, stand at Lake Street bridge, in Chicago, and look down to the Central Depot, and you have it again.

A thousand feet of this is up through granite crags, then steep slopes and perpendicular cliffs rise, one above another, to the summit. The gorge is black and narrow below, red and gray and flaring above, with crags and angular projections on the walls, which, cut in many places by side cañons, seem to be a vast wilderness of rocks. Down in these grand, gloomy depths we glide, ever listening, for the mad waters keep up their roar; ever watching, ever peering ahead, for the narrow cañon is winding, and the river is closed in so that we can see but a few hundred yards, and what there may be below we know not; but we listen for falls, and watch for rocks, or stop now and then, in the bay of a recess, to admire the gigantic scenery. And ever, as we go, there is some new pinnacle or tower, some crag or peak, some distant view of the upper plateau, some strange shaped rock, or some deep, narrow side cañon. Then we come to another broken fall, which appears more difficult than the one we ran this morning.

93

A small creek comes in on the right, and the first fall of the water is over boulders, which have been carried down by this lateral stream. We land at its mouth, and stop for an hour or two to examine the fall. It seems possible to let down with lines, at least a part of the way, from point to point, along the right hand wall. So we make a portage over the first rocks, and find footing on some boulders below. Then we let down one of the boats to the end of her line, when she reaches a corner of the projecting rock, to which one of the men clings, and steadies her, while I examine an eddy below. I think we can pass the other boats down by us, and catch them in the eddy. This is soon done and the men in the boats in the eddy pull us to their side. On the shore of this little eddy there is about two feet of gravel beach above the water. Standing on this beach, some of the men take the line of the little boat and let it drift down against another projecting angle. Here is a little shelf, on which a man from my boat climbs, and a shorter line is passed to him, and he fastens the boat to the side of the cliff. Then the second one is let down, bringing the line of the third. When the second boat is tied up, the two men standing on the beach above spring into the last boat, which is pulled up alongside of ours. Then we let down the boats, for twenty-five or thirty yards, by walking along the shelf, landing them again in the mouth of a side cañon. Just below this there is another pile of boulders, over which we make another portage. From the foot of these rocks we can climb to another shelf, forty or fifty feet above the water.

On this beach we camp for the night. We find a few sticks, which have lodged in the rocks. It is raining hard, and we have no shelter, but kindle a fire and have our supper. We sit on the rocks all night, wrapped in our ponchos, getting what sleep we can.

August 15.—This morning we find we can let down for three or four hundred yards, and it is managed in this way: We pass along the wall, by climbing from projecting point to point, sometimes near the water's edge, at other places fifty or sixty feet above, and hold the boat with a line, while two men remain aboard, and prevent her from being dashed against the rocks, and keep the line from getting caught on the wall. In two hours we have brought them all down, as far as it is possible, in this way. A few yards below, the river strikes with great violence against a projecting rock, and our boats are pulled up in a little bay above. We must now manage to pull out of this, and clear the point below. The little boat is held by the bow obliquely up the stream. We jump in, and pull out only a few strokes, and sweep clear of the dangerous rock. The other boats follow in the same manner, and the rapid is passed.

It is not easy to describe the labor of such navigation. We must prevent the waves from dashing the boats against the cliffs. Sometimes, where the river is swift, we must put a bight of rope about a rock, to prevent her being snatched from us by a wave; but where the plunge is too great, or the chute too swift, we must let her leap, and catch her below, or the undertow will drag her under the falling water, and she sinks. Where we wish to run her out a little way from shore, through a channel between rocks, we first throw in little sticks of drift wood, and watch their course, to see where we must steer, so that she will pass the channel in safety. And so we hold, and let go, and pull, and lift, and ward, among rocks, around rocks, and over rocks.

And now we go on through this solemn, mysterious way. The river is very deep, the cañon very narrow, and still obstructed, so that there is no steady flow of the stream; but the waters wheel, and roll, and boil, and we are scarcely able to determine where we can go. Now, the boat is carried to the right, perhaps close to the wall; again, she is shot into the stream, and perhaps is dragged over to the other side, where, caught in a whirlpool, she spins about. We can neither land nor run as we please. The boats are entirely unmanageable; no order in their running can be preserved; now one, now another, is ahead, each crew laboring for its own preservation. In such a place we come to another rapid. Two of the boats run it perforce. One succeeds in landing, but there, is no foot-hold by which to make a portage, and she is pushed out again into the stream. The next minute a great reflex wave fills the open compartment; she is water-logged, and drifts unmanageable. Breaker after breaker rolls over her, and one capsizes her. The men are thrown out; but they cling to the boat, and she drifts down some distance, alongside of us, and we are able to catch her. She is soon bailed out, and the men are aboard once more; but the oars are lost, so a pair from the *Emma Dean* is spared. Then for two miles we find smooth water.

Clouds are playing in the cañon today. Sometimes they roll down in great masses, filling the gorge with gloom; sometimes they hang above, from wall to wall, and cover the cañon with a roof of impending storm; and we can peer long distances up and down this cañon corridor, with its cloud roof overhead, its walls of black granite, and its river bright with the sheen of broken waters. Then, a gust of wind sweeps down a side gulch, and, making a rift in the clouds, reveals the blue heavens, and a stream of sunlight pours in. Then, the clouds drift away into the distance, and hang around crags, and peaks, and pinnacles, and towers, and walls, and cover them with a mantle, that lifts from time to time, and sets them all in sharp relief. Then, baby clouds creep out of side cañons, glide around points, and creep back again, into more distant gorges. Then, clouds, set in strata, across the cañon, with intervening vista views, to cliffs and rocks beyond. The clouds are children of the heavens, and when they play among the rocks, they lift them to the region above.

It rains! Rapidly little rills are formed above, and these soon grow into brooks, and the brooks grow into creeks, and tumble over the walls in innumerable cascades, adding their wild music to the roar of the river. When the rain ceases, the rills, brooks, and creeks run dry. The waters that fall, during a rain, on these steep rocks, are gathered at once into the river; they could scarcely be poured in more suddenly, if some vast spout ran from the clouds to the stream itself. When a storm bursts over the cañon, a side gulch is dangerous, for a sudden flood may come, and the inpouring waters will raise the river, so as to hide the rocks before your eyes.

Early in the afternoon, we discover a stream, entering from the north, a clear, beautiful creek, coming down through a gorgeous red cañon. We land, and camp on a sand beach, above its mouth, under a great, overspreading tree, with willow shaped leaves.

August 16.—We must dry our rations again today, and make oars.

The Colorado is never a clear stream, but for the past three or four days it has been raining much of the time, and the floods, which are poured over the walls, have brought down great quantities of mud, making it exceedingly turbid now. The little affluent, which we have discovered here, is a clear, beautiful creek, or river, as it would be termed in this western country, where streams are not abundant. We have named one stream, away above, in honor of the great chief of the "Bad Angels," and, as this is in beautiful contrast to that, we conclude to name it "Bright Angel."[5]

Early in the morning, the whole party starts up to explore the Bright Angel River, with the special purpose of seeking timber, from which to make oars. A couple of miles above, we find a large pine log, which has been floated down from the plateau, probably from an altitude of more than six thousand feet, but not many miles back. On its way, if must have passed over many cataracts and falls, for it bears scars in evidence of the rough usage which it has received. The men roll it on skids, and the work of sawing oars is commenced.

This stream heads away back, under a line of abrupt cliffs, that terminates the plateau, and tumbles down more than four thousand feet in the first mile or two of its course; then runs through a deep, narrow cañon, until it reaches the river.

Late in the afternoon I return, and go up a little gulch, just above this creek, about two hundred yards from camp, and discover the ruins of two or three old houses, which were originally of stone, laid in mortar. Only the foundations are left, but irregular blocks, of which the houses were constructed, lie scattered about. In one room I find an old mealing stone, deeply worn, as if it had been much used. A great deal of pottery is strewn around, and old trails, which in some places are deeply worn into the rocks, are seen.

It is ever a source of wonder to us why these ancient people sought such inaccessible places for their homes. They were, doubtless, an agricultural race, but there are no lands here, of any considerable

---

[5] Bright Angel Creek enters the Colorado just under 1,000 feet east of the modern suspension foot bridge on Bright Angel Trail. This is below the Grand Canyon Visitor Center on the South Rim.

extent, that they could have cultivated. To the west of Oraiby, one of the towns in the "Province of Tusayan," in Northern Arizona, the inhabitants have actually built little terraces along the face of the cliff, where a spring gushes out, and thus made their sites for gardens. It is possible that the ancient inhabitants of this place made their agricultural lands in the same way. But why should they seek such spots? Surely, the country was not so crowded with population as to demand the utilization of so barren a region. The only solution of the problem suggested is this: We know that, for a century or two after the settlement of Mexico, many expeditions were sent into the country now comprised in Arizona and New Mexico, for the purpose of bringing the town building people under the dominion of the Spanish government. Many of their villages were destroyed, and the inhabitants fled to regions at that time unknown; and there are traditions, among the people who inhabit the pueblos that still remain, that the cañons were these unknown lands. Maybe these buildings were erected at that time; sure it is that they have a much more modern appearance than the ruins scattered over Nevada, Utah, Colorado, Arizona, and New Mexico. Those old Spanish conquerors had a monstrous greed for gold, and a wonderful lust for saving souls. Treasures they must have; if not on earth, why, then, in heaven; and when they failed to find heathen temples, bedecked with silver, they propitiated Heaven by seizing the heathen themselves. There is yet extant a copy of a record, made by a heathen artist, to express his conception of the demands of the conquerors. In one part of the picture we have a lake, and nearby stands a priest pouring water on the head of a native. On the other side, a poor Indian has a cord about his throat. Lines run from these two groups, to a central figure, a man with beard, and full Spanish panoply. The interpretation of the picture writing is this: "Be baptized, as this saved heathen; or be hanged, as that damned heathen." Doubtless, some of these people preferred a third alternative, and, rather than be baptized or hanged, they chose to be imprisoned within these cañon walls.

August 17.—Our rations are still spoiling; the bacon is so badly injured that we are compelled to throw it away. By an accident, this morning, the saleratus[6] is lost overboard. We have now only musty flour sufficient for ten days, a few dried apples, but plenty of coffee. We must make all haste possible. If we meet with difficulties, as we have done in the cañon above, we may be compelled to give up the expedition, and try to reach the Mormon settlements to the north. Our hopes are that the worst places are passed, but our barometers are all so much injured as to be useless, so we have lost our reckoning in altitude, and know not how much descent the river has yet to make.

The stream is still wild and rapid, and rolls through a narrow channel. We make but slow progress, often landing against a wall, and climbing around some point, where we can see the river below. Although very anxious to advance, we are determined to run with great caution, lest, by another accident, we lose all our supplies. How precious that little flour has become! We divide it among the boats, and carefully store it away, so that it can be lost only by the loss of the boat itself.

We make ten miles and a half, and camp among the rocks, on the right. We have had rain, from time to time, all day, and have been thoroughly drenched and chilled; but between showers the sun shines with great power, and the mercury in our thermometers stands at 115°, so that we have rapid changes from great extremes, which are very disagreeable. It is especially cold in the rain tonight. The little canvas we have is rotten and useless; the rubber ponchos, with which we started from Green River City, have all been lost; more than half the party is without hats, and not one of us has an entire suit of clothes, and we have not a blanket apiece. So we gather drift wood, and build a fire; but after supper the rain, coming down in torrents, extinguishes it, and we sit up all night, on the rocks, shivering, and are more exhausted by the night's discomfort than by the day's toil.

August 18.—The day is employed in making portages, and we advance but two miles on our journey. Still it rains.

While the men are at work making portages, I climb up the granite to its summit, and go away back over the rust colored sandstones

---

6 Sodium bicarbonate or baking soda.

and greenish yellow shales, to the foot of the marble wall. I climb so high that the men and boats are lost in the black depths below, and the dashing river is a rippling brook; and still there is more cañon above than below. All about me are interesting geological records. The book is open, and I can read as I run. All about me are grand views, for the clouds are playing again in the gorges. But somehow I think of the nine days' rations, and the bad river, and the lesson of the rocks, and the glory of the scene is but half seen.

I push on to an angle, where I hope to get a view of the country beyond, to see, if possible, what the prospect may be of our soon running through this plateau, or, at least, of meeting with some geological change that will let us out of the granite; but, arriving at the point, I can see below only a labyrinth of deep gorges.

August 19.—Rain again this morning.

Still we are in our granite prison, and the time is occupied until noon in making a long, bad portage.

After dinner, in running a rapid, the pioneer boat is upset by a wave. We are some distance in advance of the larger boats, the river is rough and swift, and we are unable to land, but cling to the boat, and are carried downstream, over another rapid. The men in the boats above see our trouble, but they are caught in whirlpools, and are spinning about in eddies, and it seems a long time before they come to our relief. At last they do come; our boat is turned right side up, bailed out; the oars, which fortunately have floated along in company with us, are gathered up, and on we go, without even landing.

Soon after the accident the clouds break away, and we have sunshine again.

Soon we find a little beach, with just room enough to land. Here we camp, but there is no wood. Across the river, and a little way above, we see some drift wood lodged in the rocks. So we bring two boat loads over, build a huge fire, and spread everything to dry. It is the first cheerful night we have had for a week; a warm, drying fire in the midst of the camp, and a few bright stars in our patch of heavens overhead.

August 20.—The characteristics of the cañon change this morning. The river is broader, the walls more sloping, and composed of black slates, that stand on edge. These nearly vertical slates are washed out in places—that is, the softer beds are washed out between the harder, which are left standing. In this way, curious little alcoves are formed, in which are quiet bays of water, but on a much smaller scale than the great bays and buttresses of Marble cañon.

The river is still rapid, and we stop to let down with lines several times, but make greater progress as we run ten miles. We camp on the right bank. Here, on a terrace of trap, we discover another group of ruins. There was evidently quite a village on this rock. Again we find mealing stones, and much broken pottery, and up in a little natural shelf in the rock, back of the ruins, we find a globular basket, that would hold perhaps a third of a bushel. It is badly broken, and, as I attempt to take it up, it falls to pieces. There are many beautiful flint chips, as if this had been the home of an old arrow maker.

August 21.—We start early this morning, cheered by the prospect of a fine day, and encouraged, also, by the good run made yesterday. A quarter of a mile below camp the river turns abruptly to the left, and between camp and that point is very swift, running down in a long, broken chute, and piling up against the foot of the cliff, where it turns to the left. We try to pull across, so as to go down on the other side, but the waters are swift, and it seems impossible for us to escape the rock below; but, in pulling across, the bow of the boat is turned to the farther shore, so that we are swept broadside down, and are prevented, by the rebounding waters, from striking against the wall. There we toss about for a few seconds in these billows, and are carried past the danger. Below, the river turns again to the right, the cañon is very narrow, and we see in advance but a short distance. The water, too, is very swift, and there is no landing place. From around this curve there comes a mad roar, and down we are carried, with a dizzying velocity, to the head of another rapid. On either side, high over our heads, there are overhanging granite walls, and the sharp bends cut off our view, so that a few minutes will carry us into unknown waters. Away we go, on one long, winding chute. I stand on deck, supporting myself with a strap, fastened on either side to the gunwale, and the boat glides rapidly, where the water is smooth, or, striking a wave, she leaps and bounds like a thing of life, and we have a wild, exhilarating ride for ten miles, which we make in less than an hour. The excitement is so great that we forget the danger, until we hear the roar of the great fall below; then we back on our oars, and are carried slowly toward its head, and succeed in landing just above, and find that we have to make another portage. At this we are engaged until sometime after dinner.

Just here we run out of the granite![7]

Ten miles in less than half a day, and limestone walls below. Good cheer returns; we forget the storms, and the gloom, and cloud covered cañons, and the black granite, and the raging river, and push our boats from shore in great glee.

Though we are out of the granite, the river is still swift, and we wheel about a point again to the right, and turn, so as to head back in the direction from which we came, and see the granite again, with its narrow gorge and black crags; but we meet with no more great falls, or rapids. Still, we run cautiously, and stop, from time to time, to examine some places which look bad. Yet, we make ten miles this afternoon; twenty miles, in all, today.

August 22.—We come to rapids again, this morning, and are occupied several hours in passing them, letting the boats down, from rock to rock, with lines, for nearly half a mile, and then have to make a long portage. While the men are engaged in this, I climb the wall on the northeast, to a height of about two thousand five hundred feet, where I can obtain a good view of a long stretch of cañon below. Its course is to the southwest. The walls seem to rise very abruptly, for two thousand five hundred or three thousand feet, and then there is a gently sloping terrace, on each side, for two or

---

[7] Powell's description indicates they had spent the night at Waltenberg Canyon and stopped to rest ten miles below. Satellite photos clearly indicate that the latter part of the morning run was through limestone and immediately after, there is a turn to the right back into cliffs of dark stone. Twenty miles for that day would have put them at Stone Creek. After a broad turn in the river the next morning, the river, as Powell describes, turns southwest.

three miles, and again we find cliffs, one thousand five hundred or two thousand feet high. From the brink of these the plateau stretches back to the north and south, for a long distance. Away down the cañon, on the right wall, I can see a group of mountains, some of which appear to stand on the brink of the cañon. The effect of the terrace is to give the appearance of a narrow winding valley, with high walls on either side, and a deep, dark, meandering gorge down its middle. It is impossible, from this point of view, to determine whether we have granite at the bottom, or not; but, from geological considerations, I conclude that we shall have marble walls below.

After my return to the boats, we run another mile, and camp for the night.

We have made but little over seven miles today,[8] and a part of our flour has been soaked in the river again.

August 23.—Our way today is again through marble walls. Now and then we pass, for a short distance, through patches of granite, like hills thrust up into the limestone. At one of these places we have to make another portage, and, taking advantage of the delay, I go up a little stream, to the north, wading it all the way, sometimes having to plunge in to my neck; in other places being compelled to swim across little basins that have been excavated at the foot of the falls. Along its course are many cascades and springs gushing out from the rocks on either side. Sometimes a cottonwood tree grows over the water. I come to one beautiful fall, of more than a hundred and fifty feet, and climb around it to the right, on the broken rocks. Still going up, I find the cañon narrowing very much, being but fifteen or twenty feet wide; yet the walls rise on either side many hundreds of feet, perhaps thousands; I can hardly tell.

In some places the stream has not excavated its channel down vertically through the rocks, but has cut obliquely, so that one wall overhangs the other. In other places it is cut vertically above and obliquely below, or obliquely above and vertically below, so that it is impossible to see out overhead. But I can go no farther. The time

---

[8] Seven miles would have put them at Fishtail Canyon.

which I estimated it would take to make the portage has almost expired, and I start back on a round trot, wading in the creek where I must, and plunging through basins, and find the men waiting for me, and away we go on the river.

Just after dinner we pass a stream on the right, which leaps into the Colorado by a direct fall of more than a hundred feet, forming a beautiful cascade. There is a bed of very hard rock above, thirty or forty feet in thickness, and much softer beds below. The hard beds above project many yards beyond the softer, which are washed out, forming a deep cave behind the fall, and the stream pours through a narrow crevice above into a deep pool below. Around on the rocks, in the cave like chamber, are set beautiful ferns, with delicate fronds and enameled stalks. The little frondlets have their points turned down, to form spore cases. It has very much the appearance of the Maiden's hair fern, but is much larger. This delicate foliage covers the rocks all about the fountain, and gives the chamber great beauty. But we have little time to spend in admiration, so on we go.

We make fine progress this afternoon, carried along by a swift river, and shoot over the rapids, finding no serious obstructions.

The cañon walls, for two thousand five hundred or three thousand feet, are very regular, rising almost perpendicularly, but here and there set with narrow steps, and occasionally we can see away above the broad terrace, to distant cliffs.

We camp tonight in a marble cave, and find, on looking at our reckoning, we have run twenty-two miles.

August 24.—The cañon is wider today. The walls rise to a vertical height of nearly three thousand feet. In many places the river runs under a cliff, in great curves, forming amphitheaters, half dome shaped.

Though the river is rapid, we meet with no serious obstructions, and run twenty miles. It is curious how anxious we are to make up our reckoning every time we stop, now that our diet is confined to plenty of coffee, very little spoiled flour, and very few dried apples. It has come to be a race for a dinner. Still, we make such fine progress, all hands are in good cheer, but not a moment of daylight is lost.

August 25.—We make twelve miles this morning, when we come to monuments of lava, standing in the river; low rocks, mostly, but some of them shafts more than a hundred feet high. Going on down, three or four miles, we find them increasing in number. Great quantities of cooled lava and many cinder cones are seen on either side; and then we come to an abrupt cataract. Just over the fall, on the right wall, a cinder cone, or extinct volcano, with a well-defined crater, stands on the very brink of the cañon. This, doubtless, is the one we saw two or three days ago. From this volcano vast floods of lava have been poured down into the river, and a stream of the molten rock has run up the cañon, three or four miles, and down, we know not how far. Just where it poured over the cañon wall is the fall. The whole north side, as far as we can see, is lined with the black basalt, and high up on the opposite wall are patches of the same material, resting on the benches, and filling old alcoves and caves, giving to the wall a spotted appearance.[9]

The rocks are broken in two, along a line which here crosses the river, and the beds, which we have seen coming down the cañon for the last thirty miles, have dropped 800 feet, on the lower side of the line, forming what geologists call a fault. The volcanic cone stands directly over the fissure thus formed. On the side of the river opposite, mammoth springs burst out of this crevice, one or two hundred feet above the river, pouring in a stream quite equal in volume to the Colorado Chiquito.

This stream seems to be loaded with carbonate of lime, and the water, evaporating, leaves an incrustation on the rocks; and this process has been continued for a long time, for extensive deposits are noticed, in which are basins, with bubbling springs. The water is salty.

We have to make a portage here, which is completed in about three hours, and on we go.

We have no difficulty as we float along, and I am able to observe the wonderful phenomena connected with this flood of lava. The cañon was doubtless filled to a height of twelve or fifteen hundred

---

[9] The vicinity of Lava Falls Rapids.

feet, perhaps by more than one flood. This would dam the water back; and in cutting through this great lava bed, a new channel has been formed, sometimes on one side, sometimes on the other. The cooled lava, being of firmer texture than the rocks of which the walls are composed, remains in some places; in others a narrow channel has been cut, leaving a line of basalt on either side. It is possible that the lava cooled faster on the sides against the walls, and that the center ran out; but of this we can only conjecture. There are other places, where almost the whole of the lava is gone, patches of it only being seen where it has caught on the walls. As we float down, we can see that it ran out into side cañons. In some places this basalt has a fine, columnar structure, often in concentric prisms, and masses of these concentric columns have coalesced. In some places, when the flow occurred, the cañon was probably at about the same depth as it is now, for we can see where the basalt has rolled out on the sands, and, what seems curious to me, the sands are not melted or metamorphosed to any appreciable extent. In places the bed of the river is of sandstone or limestone, in other places of lava, showing that it has all been cut out again where the sandstones and limestones appear; but there is a little yet left where the bed is of lava.

What a conflict of water and fire there must have been here! Just imagine a river of molten rock, running down into a river of melted snow. What a seething and boiling of the waters; what clouds of steam rolled into the heavens!

Thirty-five miles today. Hurrah!

August 26.—The cañon walls are steadily becoming higher as we advance. They are still bold, and nearly vertical up to the terrace. We still see evidence of the eruption discovered yesterday, but the thickness of the basalt is decreasing, as we go down the stream; yet it has been reinforced at points by streams that have come down from volcanoes standing on the terrace above, but which we cannot see from the river below.

Since we left the Colorado Chiquito, we have seen no evidences that the tribe of Indians inhabiting the plateaus on either side ever come down to the river; but about eleven o'clock today we discover an Indian garden, at the foot of the wall on the right, just where a little stream, with a narrow flood plain, comes down through a side cañon. Along the valley, the Indians have planted corn, using the water which burst out in springs at the foot of the cliff, for irrigation. The corn is looking quite well, but is not sufficiently advanced to give us roasting ears; but there are some nice, green squashes. We carry ten or a dozen of these on board our boats, and hurriedly leave, not willing to be caught in the robbery, yet excusing ourselves by pleading our great want. We run down a short distance, to where we feel certain no Indians can follow; and what a kettle of squash sauce we make! True, we have no salt with which to season it, but it makes a fine addition to our unleavened bread and coffee. Never was fruit so sweet as these stolen squashes.

After dinner we push on again, making fine time, finding many rapids, but none so bad that we cannot run them with safety, and when we stop, just at dusk, and foot up our reckoning, we find we have run thirty-five miles again.

What a supper we make; unleavened bread, green squash sauce, and strong coffee. We have been for a few days on half rations, but we have no stint of roast squash.

A few days like this, and we shall be out of prison.

August 27.—This morning the river takes a more southerly direction. The dip of the rocks is to the north, and we are rapidly running into lower formations. Unless our course changes, we shall very soon run again into the granite. This gives us some anxiety. Now and then the river turns to the west, and excites hopes that are soon destroyed by another turn to the south. About nine o'clock we come to the dreaded rock. It is with no little misgiving that we see the river enter these black, hard walls. At its very entrance we have to make a portage; then we have to let down with lines past some ugly rocks. Then we run a mile or two farther, and then the rapids below can be seen.

About eleven o'clock we come to a place in the river where it seems much worse than any we have yet met in all its course. A little creek comes down from the left. We land first on the right, and clamber up over the granite pinnacles for a mile or two, but can see no way by which we can let down, and to run it would be sure destruction. After dinner we cross to examine it on the left. High above the river we can walk along on the top of the granite, which is broken off at the edge, and set with crags and pinnacles, so that it is very difficult to get a view of the river at all. In my eagerness to reach a point where I can see the roaring fall below, I go too far on the wall, and can neither advance nor retreat. I stand with one foot on a little projecting rock, and cling with my hand fixed in a little crevice. Finding I am caught here, suspended 400 feet above the river, into which I should fall if my footing fails, I call for help. The men come, and pass me a line, but I cannot let go of the rock long enough to take hold of it. Then they bring two or three of the largest oars. All this takes time which seems very precious to me; but at last they arrive. The blade of one of the oars is pushed into a little crevice in the rock beyond me, in such a manner that they can hold me pressed against the wall. Then another is fixed in such a way that I can step on it, and thus I am extricated.

Still another hour is spent in examining the river from this side, but no good view of it is obtained, so now we return to the side that was first examined, and the afternoon is spent in clambering among the crags and pinnacles, and carefully scanning the river again. We find that the lateral streams have washed boulders into the river, so as to form a dam, over which the water makes a broken fall of eighteen or twenty feet; then there is a rapid, beset with rocks, for two or three hundred yards, while, on the other side, points of the wall project into the river. Then there is a second fall below; how great, we cannot tell. Then there is a rapid, filled with huge rocks, for one or two hundred yards. At the bottom of it, from the right wall, a great rock projects quite half way across the river. It has a sloping surface extending up stream, and the water, coming down with all the momentum gained in the falls and rapids above, rolls up this inclined plane many feet, and tumbles over to the left. I decide that it is possible to let down over the first fall, then run near the right cliff to a point just above the second, where we can pull out into a little chute, and, having run over that in safety, we must pull with all our power across the stream, to avoid the great rock below.

On my return to the boat, I announce to the men that we are to run it in the morning. Then we cross the river, and go into camp for the night on some rocks, in the mouth of the little cañon.

After supper Captain Howland asks to have a talk with me. We walk up the little creek a short distance, and I soon find that his object is to remonstrate against my determination to proceed. He thinks that we had better abandon the river here. Talking with him, I learn that his brother, William Dunn, and himself have determined to go no farther in the boats. So we return to camp. Nothing is said to the other men.

For the last two days, our course has not been plotted. I sit down and do this now, for the purpose of finding where we are by dead reckoning. It is a clear night, and I take out the sextant to make observation for latitude, and find that the astronomic determination agrees very nearly with that of the plot—quite as closely as might be expected, from a meridian observation on a planet. In a direct line, we must be about forty-five miles from the mouth of the Rio Virgin. If we can reach that point, we know that there are settlements up that river about twenty miles. This forty-five miles, in a direct line, will probably be eighty or ninety in the meandering line of the river. But then we know that there is comparatively open country for many miles above the mouth of the Virgin, which is our point of destination.

As soon as I determine all this, I spread my plot on the sand, and wake Howland, who is sleeping down by the river, and show him where I suppose we are, and where several Mormon settlements are situated.

We have another short talk about the morrow, and he lies down again; but for me there is no sleep. All night long, I pace up and down a little path, on a few yards of sand beach, along by the river. Is it wise to go on? I go to the boats again, to look at our rations. I feel satisfied that we can get over the danger immediately before us; what there may be below I know not. From our outlook yesterday, on the cliffs, the cañon seemed to make another great bend to the south, and this, from our experience heretofore, means more and higher granite walls. I am not sure that we can climb out of the cañon here, and, when at the top of the wall, I know enough of the country to be certain that it is a desert of rock and sand, between this and the nearest Mormon town, which, on the most direct line, must be seventy-five miles away. True, the late rains have been favorable to us, should we go out, for the probabilities are that we shall find water still standing in holes, and, at one time, I almost conclude to leave the river. But for years I have been contemplating this trip. To leave the exploration unfinished, to say that there is a part of the cañon which I cannot explore, having already almost accomplished it, is more than I am willing to acknowledge, and I determine to go on.

I wake my brother, and tell him of Howland's determination, and he promises to stay with me; then I call up Hawkins, the cook, and he makes a like promise; then Sumner, and Bradley, and Hall, and they all agree to go on.

August 28.—At last daylight comes, and we have breakfast, without a word being said about the future. The meal is as solemn as a funeral. After breakfast, I ask the three men if they still think it best to leave us. The elder Howland thinks it is, and Dunn agrees with him. The younger Howland tries to persuade them to go on with the party, failing in which, he decides to go with his brother.

Then we cross the river. The small boat is very much disabled, and unseaworthy. With the loss of hands, consequent on the departure of the three men, we shall not be able to run all of the boats, so I decide to leave my *Emma Dean*.

Two rifles and a shotgun are given to the men who are going out. I ask them to help themselves to the rations, and take what they think to be a fair share. This they refuse to do, saying they have no fear but that they can get something to eat; but Billy, the cook, has a pan of biscuits prepared for dinner, and these he leaves on a rock.[10]

---

[10] In another day, the six remaining members of the group arrived at the mouth of the Virgin River, where Lake Mead is now. There, they learned that they had long ago been reported lost. This location has been inundated by Lake Mead since the reservoir filled after completion of Hoover Dam in 1935 (USGS website). The location where the Howlands and Dunn left is now labeled Separation Canyon.—2020

Before starting, we take our barometers, fossils, the minerals, and some ammunition from the boat, and leave them on the rocks. We are going over this place as light as possible. The three men help us lift our boats over a rock twenty-five or thirty feet high, and let them down again over the first fall, and now we are all ready to start. The last thing before leaving, I write a letter to my wife, and give it to Howland. Sumner gives him his watch, directing that it be sent to his sister, should he not be heard from again. The records of the expedition have been kept in duplicate. One set of these is given to Howland, and now we are ready. For the last time, they entreat us not to go on, and tell us that it is madness to set out in this place; that we can never get safely through it; and, further, that the river turns again to the south into the granite, and a few miles of such rapids and falls will exhaust our entire stock of rations, and then it will be too late to climb out. Some tears are shed; it is rather a solemn parting; each party thinks the other is taking the dangerous course.

My old boat left, I go on board of the *Maid of the cañon*. The three men climb a crag that overhangs the river, to watch us off. The *Maid of the cañon* pushes out. We glide rapidly along the foot of the wall, just grazing one great rock, then pull out a little into the chute of the second fall, and plunge over it. The open compartment is filled when we strike the first wave below, but we cut through it, and then the men pull with all their power toward the left wall, and swing clear of the dangerous rock below all right. We are scarcely a minute in running it, and find that, although it looked bad from above, we have passed many places that were worse.

The other boat follows without more difficulty. We land at the first practicable point below and fire our guns, as a signal to the men above that we have come over in safety. Here we remain a couple of hours, hoping that they will take the smaller boat and follow us. We are behind a curve in the cañon, and cannot see up to where we left them, and so we wait until their coming seems hopeless, and push on.

And now we have a succession of rapids and falls until noon, all of which we run in safety. Just after dinner we come to another bad place. A little stream comes in from the left, and below there is a fall, and still below another fall. Above, the river tumbles down, over and among the rocks, in whirlpools and great waves, and the waters are lashed into mad, white foam. We run along the left, above this, and soon see that we cannot get down on this side, but it seems possible to let down on the other. We pull up stream again, for two or three hundred yards, and cross. Now there is a bed of basalt on this northern side of the cañon, with a bold escarpment, that seems to be a hundred feet high. We can climb it, and walk along its summit to a point where we are just at the head of the fall. Here the basalt is broken down again, so it seems to us, and I direct the men to take a line to the top of the cliff, and let the boats down along the wall. One man remains in the boat, to keep her clear of the rocks, and prevent her line from being caught on the projecting angles. I climb the cliff, and pass along to a point just over the fall, and descend by broken rocks, and find that the break of the fall is above the break of the wall, so that we cannot land; and that still below the river is very bad, and that there is no possibility of a portage.

Without waiting further to examine and determine what shall be done, I hasten back to the top of the cliff, to stop the boats from coming down. When I arrive, I find the men have let one of them down to the head of the fall. She is in swift water, and they are not able to pull her back; nor are they able to go on with the line, as it is not long enough to reach the higher part of the cliff, which is just before them; so they take a bight around a crag. I send two men back for the other line. The boat is in very swift water, and Bradley is standing in the open compartment, holding out his oar to prevent her from striking against the foot of the cliff. Now she shoots out into the stream, and up as far as the line will permit, and then, wheeling, drives headlong against the rock, then out and back again, now straining on the line, now striking against the rock. As soon as the second line is brought, we pass it down to him; but his attention is all taken up with his own situation, and he does not see that we are passing the line to him. I stand on a projecting rock, waving my hat to gain his attention, for my voice is drowned by the roaring of the falls.

Just at this moment, I see him take his knife from its sheath, and step forward to cut the line. He has evidently decided that it is better to go over with the boat as it is, than to wait for her to be broken to pieces. As he leans over, the boat sheers again into the stream, the stem-post breaks away, and she is loose. With perfect composure Bradley seizes the great scull oar, places it in the stern rowlock, and pulls with all his power (and he is an athlete) to turn the bow of the boat downstream, for he wishes to go bow down, rather than to drift broadside on. One, two strokes he makes, and a third just as she goes over, and the boat is fairly turned, and she goes down almost beyond our sight, though we are more than a hundred feet above the river. Then she comes up again, on a great wave, and down and up, then around behind some great rocks, and is lost in the mad, white foam below. We stand frozen with fear, for we see no boat. Bradley is gone, so it seems. But now, away below, we see something coming out of the waves. It is evidently a boat. A moment more, and we see Bradley standing on deck, swinging his hat to show that he is all right. But he is in a whirlpool. We have the stempost of his boat attached to the line. How badly she may be disabled we know not.

I direct Sumner and Powell to pass along the cliff, and see if they can reach him from below. Rhodes, Hall, and myself run to the other boat, jump aboard, push out, and away we go over the falls. A wave rolls over us, and our boat is unmanageable. Another great wave strikes us, the boat rolls over, and tumbles and tosses, I know not how. All I know is that Bradley is picking us up. We soon have all right again, and row to the cliff, and wait until Sumner and Powell can come. After a difficult climb they reach us. We run two or three miles farther, and turn again to the northwest, continuing until night, when we have run out of the granite once more.

August 29.—We start very early this morning. The river still continues swift, but we have no serious difficulty, and at twelve o'clock emerge from the Grand cañon of the Colorado.

We are in a valley now, and low mountains are seen in the distance, coming to the river below. We recognize this as the Grand Wash.

A few years ago, a party of Mormons set out from St. George, Utah, taking with them a boat, and came down to the mouth of the Grand Wash, where they divided, a portion of the party crossing the river to explore the San Francisco Mountains. Three men—Hamblin, Miller, and Crosby—taking the boat, went on down the river to Callville, landing a few miles below the mouth of the Rio Virgin. We have their manuscript journal with us, and so the stream is comparatively well-known. Tonight we camp on the left bank, in a mesquite thicket.

The relief from danger, and the joy of success, are great. When he who has been chained by wounds to a hospital cot, until his canvas tent seems like a dungeon cell, until the groans of those who lie about, tortured with probe and knife, are piled up, a weight of horror on his ears that he cannot throw off, cannot forget, and until the stench of festering wounds and anæsthetic drugs has filled the air with its loathsome burthen, at last goes out into the open field, what a world he sees! How beautiful the sky; how bright the sunshine; what "floods of delirious music" pour from the throats of birds; how sweet the fragrance of earth, and tree, and blossom! The first hour of convalescent freedom seems rich recompense for all— pain, gloom, terror.

Something like this are the feelings we experience tonight. Ever before us has been an unknown danger, heavier than immediate peril. Every waking hour passed in the Grand cañon has been one of toil. We have watched with deep solicitude the steady disappearance of our scant supply of rations, and from time to time have seen the river snatch a portion of the little left, while we were ahungered. And danger and toil were endured in those gloomy depths, where oft-times the clouds hid the sky by day, and but a narrow zone of stars could be seen at night.

Only during the few hours of deep sleep, consequent on hard labor, has the roar of the waters been hushed. Now the danger is over; now the toil has ceased; now the gloom has disappeared; now the firmament is bounded only by the horizon; and what a vast expanse of constellations can be seen!

The river rolls by us in silent majesty; the quiet of the camp is sweet; our joy is almost ecstasy. We sit till long after midnight, talking of the Grand cañon, talking of home, but chiefly talking of the three men who left us. Are they wandering in those depths, unable to find a way out? Are they searching over the desert lands above for water? Or are they nearing the settlements?

August 30.—We run through two or three short, low cañons today, and on emerging from one, we discover a band of Indians in the valley below. They see us, and scamper away in most eager haste, to hide among the rocks. Although we land, and call for them to return, not an Indian can be seen.

Two or three miles farther down, in turning a short bend in the river, we come upon another camp. So near are we before they can see us that I can shout to them, and, being able to speak a little of their language, I tell them we are friends; but they all flee to the rocks, except a man, a woman, and two children. We land, and talk with them. They are without lodges, but have built little shelters of boughs, under which they wallow in the sand. The man is dressed in a hat; the woman in a string of beads only. At first they are evidently much terrified; but when I talk to them in their own language, and tell them we are friends, and inquire after people in the Mormon towns, they are soon reassured, and beg for tobacco. Of this precious article we have none to spare. Sumner looks around in the boat for something to give them, and finds a little piece of colored soap, which they receive as a valuable present, rather as a thing of beauty than as a useful commodity, however. They are either unwilling or unable to tell us anything about the Indians or white people, and so we push off, for we must lose no time.

We camp at noon under the right bank. And now, as we push out, we are in great expectancy, for we hope every minute to discover the mouth of the Rio Virgin.

Soon one of the men exclaims: "Yonder's an Indian in the river." Looking for a few minutes, we certainly do see two or three persons. The men bend to their oars, and pull toward them. Approaching, we see that there are three white men and an Indian hauling a seine, and then we discover that it is just at the mouth of the long sought river.

As we come near, the men seem far less surprised to see us than we do to see them. They evidently know who we are, and, on talking with them, they tell us that we have been reported lost long ago, and that some weeks before, a messenger had been sent from Salt Lake City, with instructions for them to watch for any fragments or relics of our party that might drift down the stream.

Our new-found friends, Mr. Asa and his two sons,[11] tell us that they are pioneers of a town that is to be built on the bank.

Eighteen or twenty miles up the valley of the Rio Virgin there are two Mormon towns, St. Joseph and St. Thomas. Tonight we dispatch an Indian to the last mentioned place, to bring any letters that may be there for us.

Our arrival here is very opportune. When we look over our store of supplies, we find about ten pounds of flour, fifteen pounds of dried apples, but seventy or eighty pounds of coffee.

August 31.—This afternoon the Indian returns with a letter, informing us that Bishop Leithhead, of St. Thomas, and two or three other Mormons are coming down with a wagon, bringing us supplies. They arrive about sundown. Mr. Asa treats us with great kindness, to the extent of his ability; but Bishop Leithhead brings in his wagon two or three dozen melons, and many other little luxuries and we are comfortable once more.

September 1.—This morning Sumner, Bradley, Hawkins, and Hall, taking on a small supply of rations, start down the Colorado with the boats. It is their intention to go to Fort Mojave, and perhaps from there overland to Los Angeles.

Captain Powell and myself return with Bishop Leithhead to St. Thomas. From St. Thomas we go to Salt Lake City.

---

[11] This was Jacob Assay (also listed as Joseph; 1823–1879), listed in the 1870 federal census as living in River Virgin, Nevada, occupation: fisherman. His two oldest sons (of ten children), were Edwin and William, also fishermen.

THE RIO VIRGIN

Here the story is continued in September of the following year 1870. (Ed.–1915)

WE have determined to continue the exploration of the cañons of the Colorado. Our last trip was so hurried, owing to the loss of rations, and the scientific instruments were so badly injured, that we are not satisfied with the results obtained, so we shall once more attempt to pass through the cañons in boats, devoting two or three years to the trip.

It will not be possible to carry in the boats sufficient supplies for the party for that length of time, so it is thought best to establish depots of supplies, at intervals of one or two hundred miles along the river.

Between Gunnison's Crossing and the foot of the Grand cañon, we know of only two points where the river can be reached—one at the Crossing of the Fathers, and another a few miles below, at the mouth of the Paria, on a route which has been explored by Jacob Hamblin, a Mormon missionary. These two points are so near each other that only one of them can be selected for the purpose above mentioned, and others must be found. We have been unable, up to this time, to obtain, either from Indians or white men, any information which will give us a clue to any other trail to the river.

At the head waters of the Sevier, we are on the summit of a great watershed. The Sevier itself flows north, and then westward, into the lake of the same name. The Rio Virgin, heading nearby, flows to the southwest, into the Colorado, sixty or seventy miles below the Grand cañon. The Kanab, also heading nearby, runs directly south, into the very heart of the Grand cañon. The Paria, also heading nearby, runs a little south of east, and enters the river at the head of Marble cañon. To the northeast from this point, other streams, which run into the Colorado, have their sources, until, forty or fifty miles away, we reach the southern branches of the Dirty Devil River, the mouth of which stream is but a short distance below the junction of the Grand and Green.

The Pouns-a'-gunt [Paunsaugunt] Plateau terminates in a point, which is bounded by a line of beautiful pink cliffs. At the foot of this plateau, on the west, the Rio Virgin and Sevier Rivers are dovetailed together, as their minute upper branches interlock. The upper surface of the plateau inclines to the northeast, so that its waters roll off into the Sevier; but from the foot of the cliffs, quite around the sharp angle of the plateau, for a dozen miles, we find numerous springs, whose waters unite to form the Kanab. But a little farther to the northeast the springs gather into streams that feed the Paria.

Here, by the upper springs of the Kanab,[1] we make a camp, and from this point we are to radiate on a series of trips, southwest, south, and east.

Jacob Hamblin,[2] who has been a missionary among the Indians for more than twenty years, has collected a number of *Kar-vav-its*, with *Chu-ar'-ru-um-peak*, their chief, and they are all camped with us. They assure us that we cannot reach the river; that we cannot make our way into the depths of the cañon, but promise to show us the springs and water pockets, which are very scarce in all this region, and to give us all the information in their power.

Here we fit up a pack train, for our bedding and instruments, and supplies are to be carried on the backs of mules and ponies.

September 5, 1870.—The several members of the party are engaged in general preparation for our trip down to the Grand cañon.

Taking with me a white man and an Indian, I start on a climb to the summit of the Pouns-a'-gunt Plateau, which rises above us on the east. Our way, for a mile or more, is over a great peat bog, that trembles under our feet, and now and then a mule sinks through the broken turf, and we are compelled to pull it out with ropes.

Passing the bog, our way is up a gulch, at the foot of the Pink Cliffs, which form the escarpment, or wall, of the great plateau. Soon

[1] Easily seen marked on maps or Google Earth.
[2] Jacob Hamblin (1819–1886) was a Mormon missionary. He showed considerable respect for the intelligence and morals of the Indians with whom he interacted (Hamblin, 1909).

we leave the gulch, and climb a long ridge, which winds around to the right toward the summit of the great table.

Two hours' riding, climbing, and clambering brings us near the top. We look below, and see clouds drifting up from the south, and rolling tumultuously toward the foot of the cliffs, beneath us. Soon, all the country below is covered with a sea of vapor—a billowy, raging, noiseless sea—and as the vapory flood still rolls up from the south, great waves dash against the foot of the cliffs and roll back; another tide comes in, is hurled back, and another and another, lashing the cliffs until the fog rises to the summit, and covers us all.

There is a heavy pine and fir forest above, beset with dead and fallen timber, and we make our way through the undergrowth to the east.

It rains! The clouds discharge their moisture in torrents, and we make for ourselves shelters of boughs, which are soon abandoned, and we stand shivering by a great fire of pine logs and boughs, which we have kindled, but which the pelting storm half extinguishes.

One, two, three, four hours of the storm, and at last it partially abates.

During this time our animals, which we have turned loose, have sought for themselves shelter under the trees, and two of them have wandered away beyond our sight. I go out to follow their tracks, and come near to the brink of a ledge of rocks, which, in the fog and mist, I suppose to be a little ridge, and I look for a way by which I can go down. Standing just here, there is a rift made in the fog below, by some current or blast of wind, which reveals an almost bottomless abyss. I look from the brink of a great precipice of more than two thousand feet; but, through the mist, the forms below are half obscured, and all reckoning of distance is lost, and it seems ten thousand feet, ten miles—any distance the imagination desires to make it.

Catching our animals, we return to the camp. We find that the little streams which come down from the plateau are greatly swollen, but at camp they have had no rain. The clouds which drifted up from the south, striking against the plateau, were lifted up into colder regions, and discharged their moisture on the summit, and against the sides of the plateau, but there was no rain in the valley below.

September 9.—We make a fair start this morning, from the beautiful meadow at the head of the Kanab, and cross the line of little hills at the headwaters of the Rio Virgin, and pass, to the south, a pretty valley, and at ten o'clock come to the brink of a great geographic bench—a line of cliffs. Behind us are cool springs, green meadows, and forest clad slopes; below us, stretching to the south, until the world is lost in blue haze, is a painted desert; not a desert plain, but a desert of rocks, cut by deep gorges, and relieved by towering cliffs and pinnacled rocks—naked rocks, brilliant in the sunlight.

By a difficult trail, we make our way down the basaltic ledge, through which innumerable streams here gather into a little river, running in a deep cañon. The river runs close to the foot of the cliffs, on the right hand side, and the trail passes along to the right. At noon we rest, and our animals feed on luxuriant grass.

Again we start, and make slow progress along a stony way. At night we camp under an overarching cliff.

September 10.—Here the river turns to the west, and our way, properly, is to the south; but we wish to explore the Rio Virgin as far as possible. The Indians tell us that the cañon narrows gradually, a few miles below, and that it will be impossible to take our animals much farther down the river. Early in the morning, I go down to examine the head of this narrow part. After breakfast, having concluded to explore the cañon for a few miles on foot, we arrange that the main party shall climb the cliff, and go around to a point eighteen or twenty miles below, where, the Indians say, the animals can be taken down by the river, and three of us set out on foot.

The Indian name of the cañon is *Pa-ru nu-weap*, or Roaring Water cañon. Between the little river and the foot of the walls, is a dense growth of willows, vines, and wild rose bushes, and, with great difficulty, we make our way through this tangled mass. It is not a wide stream—only twenty or thirty feet across in most places;

shallow, but very swift. After spending some hours in breaking our way through the mass of vegetation, and climbing rocks here and there, it is determined to wade along the stream. In some places this is an easy task, but here and there we come to deep holes, where we have to wade to our arm pits. Soon we come to places so narrow that the river fills the entire channel, and we wade perforce. In many places the bottom is a quicksand, into which we sink, and it is with great difficulty that we make progress. In some places the holes are so deep that we have to swim, and our little bundles of blankets and rations are fixed to a raft made of driftwood, and pushed before us. Now and then there is a little flood-plain, on which we can walk, and we cross and recross the stream, and wade along the channel where the water is so swift as to almost carry us off our feet, and we are in danger every moment of being swept down, until night comes on. We estimate we have traveled eight miles today. We find a little patch of flood-plain, on which there is a huge pile of driftwood and a clump of box-elders, and nearby a great stream, which bursts from the rocks—a mammoth spring.

We soon have a huge fire, our clothes are spread to dry, we make a cup of coffee, take out our bread and cheese and dried beef, and enjoy a hearty supper.

The cañon here is about twelve hundred feet deep. It has been very narrow and winding all the way down to this point.

September 11.—Wading again this morning; sinking in the quicksand, swimming the deep waters, and making slow and painful progress where the waters are swift, and the bed of the stream rocky.

The cañon is steadily becoming deeper, and, in many places, very narrow—only twenty or thirty feet wide below, and in some places no wider, and even narrower, for hundreds of feet overhead. There are places where the river, in sweeping by curves, has cut far under the rocks, but still preserving its narrow channel, so that there is an overhanging wall on one side and an inclined wall on the other. In places a few hundred feet above, it becomes vertical again, and thus the view of the sky is entirely closed. Everywhere this deep passage is dark and gloomy, and resounds with the noise of rapid waters.

At noon we are in a cañon 2,500 feet deep, and we come to a fall where the walls are broken down, and huge rocks beset the channel, on which we obtain a foothold to reach a level two hundred feet below. Here the cañon is again wider, and we find a floodplain, along which we can walk, now on this, and now on that side of the stream. Gradually the cañon widens; steep rapids, cascades, and cataracts are found along the river, but we wade only when it is necessary to cross. We make progress with very great labor, having to climb over piles of broken rocks.

Late in the afternoon, we come to a little clearing in the valley, and see other signs of civilization, and by sundown arrive at the Mormon town of Schunesburg;[3] and here we meet the train, and feast on melons and grapes.

September 12.—Our course, for the last two days, through *Pa-ru'-nu-weap* cañon, was directly to the west. Another stream comes down from the north, and unites just here at Schunesburg with the main branch of the Rio Virgin. We determine to spend a day in the exploration of this stream. The Indians call the cañon, through which it runs, *Mu-koon'-tu-weap* or Straight cañon. Entering this, we have to wade up stream; often the water fills the entire channel, and, although we travel many miles, we find no floodplain, talus, or broken piles of rock at the foot of the cliff. The walls have smooth, plain faces, and are everywhere very regular and vertical for a thousand feet or more, where they seem to break back in shelving slopes to higher altitudes; and everywhere, as we go along, we find springs bursting out at the foot of the walls, and, passing these, the river above becomes steadily smaller; the great body of water, which runs below, bursts out from beneath this great bed of red sandstone; as we go up the cañon, it comes to be but a creek, and then a brook. On the western wall of the cañon stand some buttes, towers, and high pinnacled rocks. Going up the cañon, we gain glimpses of them, here and there. Last summer, after our trip through the cañons of the Colorado, on our way from the mouth of the Virgin to Salt Lake City, these were seen as conspicuous landmarks, from a distance,

---

[3] A ghost town east of Rockville, UT in the 21st century but the old cemetery remains.

away to the southwest, of sixty or seventy miles. These tower rocks are known as the Temples of the Virgin.

Having explored this cañon nearly to its head, we return to Schunesburg, arriving quite late at night.

Sitting in camp this evening, *Chu-ar'-ru-urn-peak*, the chief of the *Kar-vav-its*, who is one of our party, tells us there is a tradition among the tribes of this country, that many years ago a great light was seen somewhere in this region by the *Pa-ru'-sha-pats*, who lived to the southwest, and that they supposed it to be a signal, kindled to warn them of the approach of the Navajos, who live beyond the Colorado River to the east. Then other signal fires were kindled on the Pine Valley Mountain, Santa Clara Mountains, and U-in-ka-ret Mountains, so that all the tribes of Northern Arizona, Southern Utah, Southern Nevada, and Southern California were warned of the approaching danger; but when the *Pa-ru'-sha-pats* came nearer, they discovered that it was a fire on one of the great Temples; and then they knew that the fire was not kindled by men, for no human being could scale the rocks. The *Tu'-mu-ur-ru-gwait'-si-gaip* or Rock Rovers, had kindled a fire to deceive the people. In the Indian language this is called *Tu'-mu-ur-ru-gwait'-si-gaip Tu-weap'*, or Rock Rovers' Land.

September 13.—We start very early this morning, for we have a long day's travel before us. Our way is across the Rio Virgin to the south. Coming to the bank of the stream here, we find a strange metamorphosis. The streams we have seen above, running in narrow channels, leaping and plunging over the rocks, raging and roaring in their course, are here united, and spread in a thin sheet several hundred yards wide, and only a few inches deep, but running over a bed of quicksand. Crossing the stream, our trail leads up a narrow cañon, not very deep, and then among the hills of golden, red, and purple shales and marls. Climbing out of the valley of the Rio Virgin, we pass through a forest of dwarf cedars, and come out at the foot of the Vermilion Cliffs. All day we follow this Indian trail toward the east, and at night camp at a great spring, known to the Indians as Yellow Rock Spring, but to the Mormons as Pipe Spring; and nearby there is a cabin in which some Mormon herders find shelter. Pipe Spring is a point just across the Utah line in Arizona,[4] and we suppose it to be about sixty miles from the river. Here the Mormons design to build a fort another year, as an outpost for protection against the Indians.

Here we discharge a number of the Indians, but take two with us for the purpose of showing us the springs, for they are very scarce, very small, and not easily found. Half a dozen are not known in a district of country large enough to make as many good sized counties in Illinois. There are no running streams, and these springs and water-pockets—that is, holes in the rocks, which hold water from shower to shower—are our only dependence for this element.

Starting, we leave behind a long line of cliffs, many hundred feet high, composed of orange and vermilion sandstones. I have named them "Vermilion Cliffs."[5] When we are out a few miles, I look back, and see the morning sun shining in splendor on their painted faces; the salient angles are on fire, and the retreating angles are buried in shade, and I gaze on them until my vision dreams, and the cliffs appear a long bank of purple clouds, piled from the horizon high into the heavens. At noon we pass along a ledge of chocolate cliffs, and, taking out our sandwiches, we make a dinner as we ride along.

Yesterday, our Indians discussed for hours the route which we should take. There is one way, farther by ten or twelve miles, with sure water; another shorter, where water is found sometimes; their conclusion was that water would be found now; and this is the way we go, yet all day long we are anxious about it. To be out two days, with only the water that can be carried in two small kegs, is to have our animals suffer greatly. At five o'clock we come to the spot, and there is a huge water-pocket, containing several barrels. What a relief! Here we camp for the night.

September 15.—Up at daybreak, for it is a long day's march to the next water. They say we must "run very hard" to reach it by dark.

---

[4] See Pipe Spring National Monument.
[5] Vermilion Cliffs is now a National Monument of weird, beautiful, and colorful rock formations.

Our course is to the south. From Pipe Spring we can see a mountain, and I recognize it as the one seen last summer from a cliff overlooking the Grand cañon; and I wish to reach the river just behind the mountain. There are Indians living in the group, of which it is the highest, whom I wish to visit on the way. These mountains are of volcanic origin, and we soon come to ground that is covered with fragments of lava. The way becomes very difficult. We have to cross deep ravines, the heads of cañons that run into the Grand cañon. It is curious now to observe the knowledge of our Indians. There is not a trail but what they know; every gulch and every rock seems familiar. I have prided myself on being able to grasp and retain in my mind the topography of a country; but these Indians put me to shame. My knowledge is only general, embracing the more important features of a region that remains as a map engraved on my mind; but theirs is particular. They know every rock and every ledge, every gulch and cañon, and just where to wind among these to find a pass; and their knowledge is unerring. They cannot describe a country to you, but they can tell you all the particulars of a route.

I have but one pony for the two, and they were to ride "turn about"; but *Chu-ar'-ru-urn-peak*, the chief, rides, and Shuts, the one-eyed, bare-legged, merry-faced pigmy, walks, and points the way with a slender cane; then leaps and bounds by the shortest way, and sits down on a rock and waits demurely until we come, always meeting us with a jest, his face a rich mine of sunny smiles.

At dusk we reach the water-pocket. It is in a deep gorge, on the flank of this great mountain. During the rainy season the water rolls down the mountain side, plunging over precipices, and excavates a deep basin in the solid rock below. This basin, hidden from the sun, holds water the year round.

September 16.—This morning, while the men are packing the animals, I climb a little mountain near camp, to obtain a view of the country. It is a huge pile of volcanic scoria, loose and light as cinders from a forge, which give way under my feet, and I climb with great labor; but reaching the summit, and looking to the southeast, I see once more the labyrinth of deep gorges that flank the Grand cañon;

in the multitude, I cannot determine whether it be in view or not. The memories of grand and awful months spent in their deep, gloomy solitudes come up, and I live that life over again for a time.

I supposed, before starting, that I could get a good view of the great mountain from this point; but it is like climbing a chair to look at a castle. I wish to discover some way by which it can be ascended, as it is my intention to go to the summit before I return to the settlements. There is a cliff near the summit, and I do not see the way yet. Now down I go, sliding on the cinders, making them rattle and clang.

The Indians say we are to have a short ride today, and that we will reach an Indian village, situated by a good spring. Our way is across the spurs that put out from the great mountain, as we pass it to the left.

Up and down we go, across deep ravines, and the fragments of lava clank under our horses' feet; now among cedars, now among pines, and now across mountain side glades. At one o'clock we descend into a lovely valley, with a carpet of waving grass; sometimes there is a little water in the upper end of it, and, during some seasons, the Indians we wish to find are encamped here. *Chu-ar'-ru-um-peak* rides on to find them, and to say we are friends, otherwise they would run away, or propose to fight us, should we come without notice. Soon we see *Chu-ar'-ru-um-peak* riding at full speed, and hear him shouting at the top of his voice, and away in the distance are two Indians, scampering up the mountain side. One stops; the other still goes on, and is soon lost to view. We ride up, and find *Chu-ar'-ru-um-peak* talking with the one who had stopped. It is one of the ladies resident in these mountain glades; she is evidently paying taxes, Godiva like.[6] She tells us that her people are at the spring; that it is only two hours' ride; that her good master has gone on to tell them we are coming, and that she is harvesting seeds.

We sit down and eat our luncheon, and share our biscuit with the woman of the mountains; then on we go, over a divide between two

---

[6] In other words, naked.

rounded peaks. I send the party on to the village, and climb the peak on the left, riding my horse to the upper limit of trees, and then tugging up afoot. From this point I can see the Grand cañon, and know where I am. I can see the Indian village, too, in a grassy valley, embosomed in the mountains, the smoke curling up from their fires; my men are turning out their horses, and a group of natives stand around. Down the mountain I go, and reach camp at sunset.

After supper we put some cedar boughs on the fire, the dusky villagers sit around, and we have a smoke and a talk. I explain the object of my visit, and assure them of my friendly intentions. Then I ask them about a way down into the cañon. They tell me that years ago, a way was discovered by which parties could go down, but that no one has attempted it for a long time; that it is a very difficult and very dangerous undertaking to reach the "Big Water." Then I inquire about the *Shi'-vwits*, a tribe that lives about the springs on the mountain sides and cañon cliffs to the southwest. They say that their village is now about thirty miles away, and promise to send a messenger for them tomorrow morning.

Having finished our business for the evening, I ask if there is a *tu-gwi'-na-gunt* in camp: that is, if there is any one present who is skilled in relating their mythology. *Chu-ar'-ru-um-peak* says *To-mor'-ro-un-ti-kai*, the chief of these Indians, is a very noted man for his skill in this matter; but they both object, by saying that the season for *tu-gwi'-nai* has not yet arrived. But I had anticipated this, and soon some members of the party come with pipes and tobacco, a large kettle of coffee, and a tray of biscuits, and, after sundry ceremonies of pipe lighting and smoking, we all feast, and, warmed up by this, to them, unusual good living, it is decided that the night shall be spent in relating mythology. I ask *To-mor'-ro-un-ti-kai* to tell us about the *So'-kus Wai'-un-ats*, or One Two Boys, and to this he agrees.

The long winter evenings of an Indian camp are usually devoted to the relation of mythological stories, which purport to give a history of an ancient race of animal gods. The stories are usually told by some old man, assisted by others of the party, who take secondary parts, while the members of the tribe gather about, and make comments, or receive impressions from the morals which are enforced by the story teller, or, more properly, story tellers; for the exercise partakes somewhat of the nature of a theatrical performance.

THE SO'-KUS WAI'-UN-ATS.

Tum-pwi-nai'-ro-gwi-nump, he who had a stone shirt, killed *Si-kor*, the Crane, and stole his wife, and seeing that she had a child, and thinking it would he an incumbrance to them on their travels, he ordered her to kill it. But the mother, loving the babe, hid it under her dress, and carried it away to its grandmother. And Stone Shirt carried his captured bride to his own land.

In a few years the child grew to be a fine lad, under the care of his grandmother, and was her companion wherever she went.

One day they were digging flag roots, on the margin of the river, and putting them in a heap on the bank. When they had been at work a little while, the boy perceived that the roots came up with greater ease than was customary, and he asked the old woman the cause of this, but she did not know; and, as they continued their work, still the reeds came up with less effort, at which their wonder increased, until the grandmother said, "Surely, some strange thing is about to transpire." Then the boy went to the heap, where they had been placing the roots, and found that someone had taken them away, and he ran back, exclaiming, "Grandmother, did you take the roots away?" And she answered, "No, my child; perhaps some ghost has taken them off; let us dig no more; come away." But the boy was not satisfied, as he greatly desired to know what all this meant; so he searched about for a time, and at length found a man sitting under a tree, whom he taunted with being a thief, and threw mud and stones at him, until he broke the stranger's leg, who answered not the boy, nor resented the injuries he received, but remained silent and sorrowful; and, when his leg was broken, he tied it up in sticks, and bathed it in the river, and sat down again under the tree, and beckoned the boy to approach. When the lad came near, the stranger told him he had something of great importance to reveal. "My son," said he, "did that old woman ever tell you about your father and mother?" "No," answered the boy; "I have never heard of

128

them." "My son, do you see these bones scattered on the ground? Whose bones are these?" "How should I know?" answered the boy. "It may be that some elk or deer has been killed here." "No," said the old man. "Perhaps they are the bones of a bear;" but the old man shook his head. So the boy mentioned many other animals, but the stranger still shook his head, and finally said, "These are the bones of your father; Stone Shirt killed him, and left him to rot here on the ground, like a wolf." And the boy was filled with indignation against the slayer of his father. Then the stranger asked, "Is your mother in yonder lodge?" and the boy replied, "No." "Does your mother live on the banks of this river?" and the boy answered, "I don't know my mother; I have never seen her; she is dead." "My son," replied the stranger, "Stone Shirt, who killed your father, stole your mother, and took her away to the shore of a distant lake, and there she is his wife today." And the boy wept bitterly, and while the tears filled his eyes so that he could not see, the stranger disappeared. Then the boy was filled with wonder at what he had seen and heard, and malice grew in his heart against his father's enemy. He returned to the old woman, and said, "Grandmother, why have you lied to me about my father and mother?" and she answered not, for she knew that a ghost had told all to the boy. And the boy fell upon the ground weeping and sobbing, until he fell into a deep sleep, when strange things were told him.

His slumber continued three days and three nights, and when he awoke, he said to his grandmother: "I am going away to enlist all nations in my fight;" and straightway he departed.

(Here the boy's travels are related with many circumstances concerning the way he was received by the people, all given in a series of conversations, very lengthy, so they will be omitted.)

Finally he returned in advance of the people whom he had enlisted, bringing with him *Shin-au'-av*, the wolf, and *To-go'-av*, the rattlesnake. When the three had eaten food, the boy said to the old woman: "Grandmother, cut me in two!" But she demurred, saying she did not wish to kill one whom she loved so dearly. "Cut me in two!" demanded the boy; and he gave her a stone ax, which he had brought from a distant country, and with a manner of great authority he again commanded her to cut him in two. So she stood before him, and severed him in twain, and fled in terror. And lo! each part took the form of an entire man, and the one beautiful boy appeared as two, and they were so much alike no one could tell them apart.

When the people or natives, whom the boy had enlisted, came pouring into the camp, *Shin-au'-av* and *To-go'-av* were engaged in telling them of the wonderful thing that had happened to the boy, and that now there were two; and they all held it to be an augury of a successful expedition to the land of Stone Shirt. And they started on their journey.

Now the boy had been told in the dream of his three days' slumber, of a magical cup, and he had brought it home with him from his journey among the nations, and the *So'-kus Wai'-un-ats* carried it between them, filled with water. *Shin-au'-av* walked on their right, and *To-go'-av* on their left, and the nations followed in the order in which they had been enlisted. There was a vast number of them, so that when they were stretched out in line it was one day's journey from the front to the rear of the column.

When they had journeyed two days, and were far out on the desert, all the people thirsted, for they found no water, and they fell down upon the sand, groaning, and murmuring that they had been deceived, and they cursed the One-Two.

But the *So'-kus Wai'-un-ats* had been told in the wonderful dream of the suffering which would be endured, and that the water which they carried in the cup was only to be used in dire necessity; and the brothers said to each other: "Now the time has come for us to drink the water." And when one had quaffed of the magical bowl, he found it still full; and he gave it to the other to drink, and still it was full; and the One-Two gave it to the people, and one after another did they all drink, and still the cup was full to the brim.

But *Shin-au'-av* was dead, and all the people mourned, for he was a great mam

The brothers held the cup over him, and sprinkled him with water, when he arose and said: "Why do you disturb me? I did have a vision of mountain brooks and meadows, of cane where honey-dew was plenty." They gave him the cup, and he drank also; but when he had finished there was none left. Refreshed and rejoicing they proceeded on their journey.

The next day, being without food, they were hungry, and all were about to perish; and again they murmured at the brothers, and cursed them. But the *So'-kus Wai'-un-ats* saw in the distance an antelope, standing on an eminence in the plain, in bold relief against the sky; and *Shin-au'-av* knew it was the wonderful antelope with many eyes, which Stone Shirt kept for his watchman; and he proposed to go and kill it, but *To-go'-av* demurred, and said: "It were better that I should go, for he will see you, and run away." But the *So'-kus Wai'-un-ats* told *Shin-au'-av* to go; and he started in a direction away to the left of where the antelope was standing, that he might make a long detour about some hills, and come upon him from the other side. *To-go'-av* went a little way from camp, and called to the brothers: "Do you see me?" and they answered they did not. "Hunt for me;" and while they were hunting for him, the rattlesnake said: "I can see you; you are doing"—so and so, telling them what they were doing; but they could not find him.

Then the rattlesnake came forth, declaring: "Now you know I can see others, and that I cannot be seen when I so desire. *Shin-au'-av* cannot kill that antelope, for he has many eyes, and is the wonderful watchman of Stone Shirt; but I can kill him, for I can go where he is, and he cannot see me." So the brothers were convinced, and permitted him to go; and he went and killed the antelope. When *Shin-au'-av* saw it fall, he was very angry, for he was extremely proud of his fame as a hunter, and anxious to have the honor of killing this famous antelope, and he ran up with the intention of killing *To-go'-av*; but when he drew near, and saw the antelope was fat, and would make a rich feast for the people, his anger was appeased. "What matters it," said he, "who kills the game, when we can all eat it?"

So all the people were fed in abundance, and they proceeded on their journey.

The next day the people again suffered for water, and the magical cup was empty; but the *So'-kus Wai'-un-ats*, having been told in their dream what to do, transformed themselves into doves, and flew away to a lake, on the margin of which was the home of Stone Shirt.

Coming near to the shore, they saw two maidens bathing in the water; and the birds stood and looked, for the maidens were very beautiful. Then they flew into some bushes, nearby, to have a nearer view, and were caught in a snare which the girls had placed for intrusive birds. The beautiful maidens came up, and, taking the birds out of the snare, admired them very much, for they had never seen such birds before. They carried them to their father, Stone Shirt, who said: "My daughters, I very much fear these are spies from my enemies, for such birds do not live in our land;" and he was about to throw them into the fire, when the maidens besought him, with tears, that he would not destroy their beautiful birds; but he yielded to their entreaties with much misgiving. Then they took the birds to the shore of the lake, and set them free.

When the birds were at liberty once more, they flew around among the bushes, until they found the magical cup which they had lost, and taking it up, they carried it out into the middle of the lake and settled down upon the water, and the maidens, supposed they were drowned.

The birds, when they had filled their cup, rose again, and went back to the people in the desert, where they arrived just at the right time to save them with the cup of water, from which each drank; and yet it was full until the last was satisfied, and then not a drop remained.

The brothers reported that they had seen Stone Shirt and his daughters.

The next day they came near to the home of the enemy, and the brothers, in proper person, went out to reconnoitre. Seeing a woman gleaning seeds, they drew near, and knew it was their mother, whom Stone Shirt had stolen from *Si-kor'*, the crane. They told her they were her sons, but she denied it, and said she had never had but one son; but the boys related to her their history, with the origin of the two from one, and she was convinced. She tried to dissuade them from making war upon Stone Shirt, and told them that no arrow could possibly penetrate his armor, and that he was a great warrior, and had no other delight than in killing his enemies, and that his daughters also were furnished with magical bows and arrows, which they could shoot so fast that the arrows would fill the air like a cloud, and that it was not necessary for them to take aim, for their missiles went where they willed; they *thought* the arrows to the hearts of their enemies; and thus the maidens could kill the whole of the people before a common arrow could be shot by a common person. But the boys told her what the spirit had said in the long dream, and had promised that Stone Shirt should be killed. They told her to go down to the lake at dawn, so as not to be endangered by the battle.

During the night, the *So'-kus Wai'-un-ats* transformed themselves into mice, and proceeded to the home of Stone Shirt, and found the magical bows and arrows that belonged to the maidens, and with their sharp teeth they cut the sinew on the backs of the bows, and nibbled the bow strings, so that they were worthless; while *To-go'-av* hid himself under a rock nearby.

When dawn came into the sky, *Tum-pwi-nai'-ro-gwi-nump*, the Stone Shirt man, arose and walked out of his tent, exulting in his strength and security, and sat down upon the rock under which *To-go'-av* was hiding; and he, seeing his opportunity, sunk his fangs into the flesh of the hero. Stone Shirt sprang high into the air, and called to his daughters that they were betrayed, and that the enemy was near; and they seized their magical bows, and their quivers filled with magical arrows, and hurried to his defense. At the same time, all the nations who were surrounding the camp rushed down to battle. But the beautiful maidens, finding their weapons were destroyed, waved back their enemies, as if they would parley; and, standing for a few moments over the body of their slain father, sang the death song, and danced the death dance, whirling in giddy circles about the dead hero, and wailing with despair, until they sank down and expired.

The conquerors buried the maidens by the shores of the lake; but *Tum-pwi-nai'-ro-gwi-nump* was left to rot, and his bones to bleach on the sands, as he had left *Si-kor'*.

There is this proverb among the Utes: "Do not murmur when you suffer in doing what the spirits have commanded, for a cup of water is provided." And another: "What matters it who kills the game, when we can all eat of it."

It is long after midnight when the performance is ended. The story itself was interesting, though I had heard it many times before; but never, perhaps, under circumstances more effective. Stretched beneath tall, sombre pines; a great camp fire, and by the fire, men, old, wrinkled, and ugly; deformed, blear eyed, wry faced women; lithe, stately young men; pretty but simpering maidens, naked children, all intently listening, or laughing and talking at times, their strange faces and dusky forms lit up with the glare of the pine-knot fire. All the circumstances conspired to make it a scene strange and weird. One old man, the sorcerer or medicine-man of the tribe, peculiarly impressed me. Now and then he would interrupt the play for the purpose of correcting the speakers, or impressing the moral of the story with a strange dignity and impressiveness that seemed to pass to the very border of the ludicrous; yet at no time did it make me smile.

The story is finished, but there is yet time for an hour or two's sleep. I take *Chu-ar'-ru-um-peak* to one side for a talk. The three men who left us in the cañon last year found their way up the lateral gorge, by which they went into the *Shi'-vwits* Mountains, lying west of us, where they met with the Indians, and camped with them one or two nights, and were finally killed. I am anxious to learn the circumstances, and as the people of the tribe who committed the deed live but a little way from and are intimate with these people, I ask *Chu-ar'-ru-um-peak* to make inquiry for me. Then we go to bed.

September 17.—Early this morning the Indians come up to our camp. They have concluded to send out a young man after the *Shi'-vwits*. The runner fixes his moccasins, puts some food in a sack and water in a little wicker work jug, straps them on his back, and starts at a good round pace.

We have concluded to go down the cañon, hoping to meet the *Shi'-vwits* on our return. Soon we are ready to start, leaving the camp and pack animals in charge of the two Indians who came with us. As we move out, our new guide comes up, a blear eyed, weazen faced, quiet old man, with his bow and arrows in one hand, and a small cane in the other. These Indians all carry canes with a crooked handle, they say to kill rattlesnakes, and to pull rabbits from their holes. The valley is high up in the mountain, and we descend from it, by a rocky, precipitous trail, down, down, down for two long, weary hours, leading our ponies and stumbling over the rocks. At last we are at the foot of the mountain, standing on a little knoll, from which we can look into a cañon below. Into this we descend, and then we follow it for miles, clambering down and still down. Often we cross beds of lava, that have been poured into the cañon by lateral channels, and these angular fragments of basalt make the way very rough for the animals.

About two o'clock the guide halts us with his wand, and springing over the rocks he is lost in a gulch. In a few minutes he returns, and tells us there is a little water below in a pocket. It is vile and stinking, and our ponies refuse to drink it. We pass on, still ever descending. A mile or two from the water basin we come to a precipice, more than a thousand feet to the bottom. There is a cañon running at a greater depth, and at right angles to this, into which this enters by the precipice; and this second cañon is a lateral one to the greater one, in the bottom of which we are to find the river. Searching about, we find a way by which we can descend along the shelves, and steps, and piles of broken rocks.

We start leading our ponies; a wall upon our left; unknown depths on our right. At places our way is along shelves so narrow, or so sloping, that I ache with fear lest a pony should make a misstep, and knock a man over the cliffs with him. Now and then we start the loose rocks under our feet, and over the cliffs they go, thundering down, down, as the echoes roll through distant cañons. At last we pass along a level shelf for some distance, then we turn to the right, and zigzag down a steep slope to the bottom. Now we pass along this lower cañon, for two or three miles, to where it terminates in the

Grand cañon, as the other ended in this, only the river is 1,800 feet below us, and it seems, at this distance, to be but a creek. Our withered guide, the human pickle, seats himself on a rock, and seems wonderfully amused at our discomfiture, for we can see no way by which to descend to the river. After some minutes, he quietly rises, and, beckoning us to follow, he points out a narrow sloping shelf on the right, and this is to be our way. It leads along the cliff, for half a mile, to a wider bench beyond, which, he says, is broken down on the other side in a great slide, and there we can get to the river. So we start out on the shelf; it is so steep we can hardly stand on it, and to fall, or slip, is to go—don't look and see!

It is soon manifest that we cannot get the ponies along the ledge. The storms have washed it down, since our guide was here last, years ago. One of the ponies has gone so far that we cannot turn him back until we find a wider place, but at last we get him off. With part of the men, I take the horses back to the place where there are a few bushes growing, and turn them loose; in the meantime the other men are looking for some way by which we can get down to the river. When I return, one, Captain Bishop, has found a way, and gone down. We pack bread, coffee, sugar, and two or three blankets among us, and set out. It is now nearly dark, and we cannot find the way by which the captain went, and an hour is spent in fruitless search. Two of the men go away around an amphitheater, more than a fourth of a mile, and start down a broken chasm that faces us, who are behind. These walls, that are vertical, or nearly so, are often cut by chasms, where the showers run down, and the top of these chasms will be back a distance from the face of the wall, and the bed of the chasm will slope down, with here and there a fall. At other places, huge rocks have fallen, and block the way. Down such a one the two men start. There is a curious plant growing out from the crevices of the rock. A dozen stems will start from one root, and grow to the length of eight or ten feet, and not throw out a branch or twig, but these stems are thickly covered with leaves. Now and then the two men come to a bunch of dead stems, and make a fire to mark for us their way and progress.

In the meantime we find such a gulch, and start down, but soon come to the "jumping off place," where we can throw a stone, and hear it faintly striking, away below. We fear that we shall have to stay here, clinging to the rocks until daylight. Our little Indian gathers a few dry stems, ties them into a bundle, lights one end, and holds it up. The others do the same, and with these torches we find a way out of trouble. Helping each other, holding torches for each other, one clinging to another's hand until we can get footing, then supporting the other on his shoulders, so we make our passage into the depths of the cañon. And now Captain Bishop has kindled a huge fire of driftwood, on the bank of the river. This, and the fires in the gulch opposite, and our own flaming torches, light up little patches, that make more manifest the awful darkness below. Still, on we go, for an hour or two, and at last we see Captain Bishop coming up the gulch, with a huge torch-light on his shoulders. He looks like a fiend, waving brands and lighting the fires of hell, and the men in the opposite gulch are imps, lighting delusive fires in inaccessible crevices, over yawning chasms; our own little Indian is surely the king of wizards, so I think, as I stop for a few moments on a rock to rest. At last we meet Captain Bishop, with his flaming torch, and, as he has learned the way, he soon pilots us to the side of the great Colorado. We are hungry and athirst, almost to starvation. Here we lie down on the rocks and drink, just a mouthful or so, as we dare; then we make a cup of coffee, and, spreading our blankets on a sand beach, the roaring Colorado lulls us to sleep.

September 18.—We are in the Grand cañon, by the side of the Colorado, more than six thousand feet below our camp on the mountain side, which is eighteen miles away; but the miles of horizontal distance represent but a small part of the day's labor before us. It is the mile of altitude we must gain that makes it a herculean task. We are up early; a little bread and coffee, and we look about us. Our conclusion is that we can make this a depot of supplies, should it be necessary; that we can pack our rations to the point where we left our animals last night, and that we can employ Indians to bring them down to the water's edge.

On a broad shelf, we find the ruins of an old stone house, the walls of which are broken down, and we can see where the ancient people who lived here—a race more highly civilized than the present—had made a garden, and used a great spring, that comes out of the rocks, for irrigation. On some rocks nearby we discover some curious etchings. Still, searching about, we find an obscure trail up the cañon wall, marked, here and there, by steps which have been built in the loose rock, elsewhere hewn stairways, and we find a much easier way to go up than that by which we came down in the darkness last night. Coming to the top of the wall, we catch our horses, and start. Up the cañon our jaded ponies toil, and we reach the second cliff; up this we go, by easy stages, leading the animals. Now we reach the stinking water-pocket; our ponies have had no water for thirty hours, and are eager even for this foul fluid. We carefully strain a kettleful for ourselves, then divide what is left between them—two or three gallons for each; but this does not satisfy them, and they rage around, refusing to eat the scanty grass. We boil our kettle of water, and skim it; straining, boiling, and skimming makes it a little better, for it was full of loathsome, wriggling larvæ, with huge black heads. But plenty of coffee takes away the bad smell, and so modifies the taste that most of us can drink, though our little Indian seems to prefer the original mixture. We reach camp about sunset, and are glad to rest.

September 19.—We are tired and sore, and must rest a day with our Indian neighbors. During the inclement season they live in shelters, made of boughs, or bark of the cedar, which they strip off in long shreds. In this climate, most of the year is dry and warm, and during such time they do not care for shelter. Clearing a small, circular space of ground, they bank it around with brush and sand, and wallow in it during the day, and huddle together in a heap at night, men, women, and children; buckskin, rags, and sand. They wear very little clothing, not needing much in this lovely climate.

Altogether, these Indians are more nearly in their primitive condition than any others on the continent with whom I am acquainted.

They have never received anything from the Government, and are too poor to tempt the trader, and their country is so nearly inaccessible that the white man never visits them. The sunny mountain side is covered with wild fruits, nuts, and native grains, upon which they subsist. The *oose*, the fruit of the yucca, or Spanish bayonet, is rich, and not unlike the paw-paw of the valley of the Ohio. They eat it raw, and also roast it in the ashes. They gather the fruits of a cactus plant, which is rich and luscious, and eat them as grapes, or from them express the juice, making the dry pulp into cakes, and saving them for winter; the wine they drink about their camp fires, until the midnight is merry with the revelries.

They gather the seeds of many plants, as sunflowers, goldenrods, and grasses. For this purpose, they have large conical baskets, which hold two or more bushels. The women carry them on their backs, suspended from their foreheads by broad straps, and with a smaller one in the left hand, and a willow woven fan in the right, they walk among the grasses, and sweep the seed into the smaller basket, which is emptied, now and then, into the larger, until it is full of seeds and chaff; then they winnow out the chaff and roast the seeds. They roast these curiously; they put the seeds, with a quantity of red hot coals, into a willow tray, and, by rapidly and dexterously shaking and tossing them, keep the coals aglow, and the seeds and tray from burning. As if by magic, so skilled are the crones in this work, they roll the seeds to one side of the tray, as they are roasted, and the coals to the other. Then they grind the seeds into a fine flour, and make it into cakes and mush.

It is a merry sight, sometimes, to see the women grinding at the mill. For a mill, they use a large flat rock, lying on the ground, and another small cylindrical one in their hands. They sit prone on the ground, hold the large flat rock between the feet and legs, then fill their laps with seeds, making a hopper to the mill with their dusky legs, and grind by pushing the seeds across the larger rock, where it drops into a tray. I have seen a group of women grinding together, keeping time to a chant, or gossiping and chatting, while the younger lassies would jest and chatter, and make the pine woods merry with their laughter. Mothers carry their babes curiously in baskets. They make a wicker board, by plaiting willows, and sew a buckskin cloth to either edge, and this is fulled in the middle, so as to form a sack, closed at the bottom. At the top, they make a wicker shade, like "my grandmother's sun bonnet," and, wrapping the little one in a wild cat robe, place it in the basket, and this they carry on their backs, strapped over the forehead, and the little brown midgets are ever peering over their mother's shoulders. In camp, they stand the basket against the trunk of a tree, or hang it to a limb.

There is little game in the country, yet they get a mountain sheep now and then, or a deer, with their arrows, for they are not yet supplied with guns. They get many rabbits, sometimes with arrows, sometimes with nets. They make a net of twine, made of the fibers of a native flax. Sometimes this is made a hundred yards in length, and is placed in a half circular position, with wings of sage brush. They have a circle hunt, and drive great numbers of rabbits into the snare, where they are shot with arrows. Most of their bows are made of cedar, but the best are made of the horns of mountain sheep. These are taken, soaked in water, until quite soft, cut into long thin strips, and glued together, and are then quite elastic. During the autumn, grasshoppers are very abundant. When cold weather sets in, these insects are numbed, and can be gathered by the bushel. At such a time, they dig a hole in the sand, heat stones in a fire nearby, put some in the bottom of the hole, put on a layer of grasshoppers, then a layer of hot stones, and continue this, until they put bushels on to roast. There they are left until cool, when they are taken out, thoroughly dried, and ground into meal. Grasshopper gruel, or grasshopper cake, is a great * treat.

Their lore consists in a mass of traditions, or mythology. It is very difficult to induce them to tell it to white men; but the old Spanish priests, in the days of the conquest of New Mexico, have spread among the Indians of this country many Bible stories, which the Indians are usually willing to tell. It is not always easy to recognize them, the Indian mind being a strange receptacle for such stories, and they are apt to sprout new limbs. Maybe much of their added quaintness is due to the way in which they were told by the "fathers." But in a confidential way, while you are alone, or when you are admitted to their camp fire on a winter night, you will hear the stories of their mythology. I believe that the greatest mark of friendship, or confidence, that an Indian can give, is to tell you his religion. After one has so talked with me, I should ever trust him; and I feel on very good terms with these Indians, since our experience of the other night.

A knowledge of the watering places, and of the trails and passes, is considered of great importance, and is necessary, to give standing to a chief.

This evening, the Shi'-vwits, for whom we have sent, come in, and, after supper, we hold a long council. A blazing fire is built, and around this we sit—the Indians living here, the Shi'-vwits, Jacob Hamblin, and myself. This man, Hamblin, speaks their language well, and has a great influence over all the Indians in the region round about. He is a silent, reserved man, and when he speaks, it is in a slow, quiet way, that inspires great awe. His talk is so low that they must listen attentively to hear, and they sit around him in deathlike silence. When he finishes a measured sentence, the chief repeats it, and they all give a solemn grunt. But, first, I fill my pipe, light it, and take a few whiffs, then pass it to Hamblin; he smokes, and gives it to the man next, and so it goes around. When it has passed the chief, he takes out his own pipe, fills, and lights it, and passes it around after mine. I can smoke my own pipe in turn, but, when the Indian pipe comes around, I am nonplussed. It has a large stem, which has, at some time, been broken, and now there is a buckskin rag wound around it, and tied with sinew, so that the end of the stem is a huge mouthful, and looks like the burying ground of old dead spittle, venerable for a century. To gain time, I refill it, then engage in very earnest conversation, and, all unawares, I pass it to my neighbor unlighted.

I tell the Indians that I wish to spend some months in their country during the coming year, and that I would like them to treat me as a friend. I do not wish to trade; do not want their lands. Heretofore I have found it very difficult to make the natives understand my object, but the gravity of the Mormon missionary helps me much. I tell them that all the great and good white men are anxious to know very many things; that they spend much time in learning, and that the greatest man is he who knows the most. They want to know all about the mountains and the valleys, the rivers and the cañons, the beasts, and birds, and snakes. Then I tell them of many Indian tribes, and where they live; of the European nations; of the Chinese, of Africans, and all the strange things about them that come to my mind. I tell them of the ocean, of great rivers and high mountains, of strange beasts and birds. At last I tell them I wish to learn about their cañons and mountains, and about themselves, to tell other men at home; and that I want to take pictures of everything, and show them to my friends. All this occupied much time, and the matter and manner made a deep impression.

Then their chief replies: "Your talk is good, and we believe what you say. We believe in Jacob, and look upon you as a father. When you are hungry, you may have our game. You may gather our sweet fruits. We will give you food when you come to our land. We will show you the springs, and you may drink; the water is good. We will be friends, and when you come we will be glad. We will tell the Indians who live on the other side of the great river that we have seen *Ka'-pu-rats*, and he is the Indians' friend. We will tell them he is Jacob's friend. We are very poor. Look at our women and children; they are naked. We have no horses; we climb the rocks, and our feet are sore. We live among rocks, and they yield little food and many thorns. When the cold moons come, our children are hungry. We have not much to give; you must not think us mean. You are wise; we have heard you tell strange things. We are ignorant. Last year we killed three white men. Bad men said they were our enemies. They told great lies. We thought them true. We were mad; it made us big fools. We are very sorry. Do not think of them, it is done; let us be friends. We are ignorant—like little children in understanding compared with you. When we do wrong, do not get mad, and be like children too.

"When white men kill our people, we kill them. Then they kill more of us. It is not good. We hear that the white men are a great number. When they stop killing us, there will be no Indian left to bury the dead. We love our country; we know not other lands. We hear that other lands are better; we do not know. The pines sing, and we are glad. Our children play in the warm sand; we hear them sing, and are glad. The seeds ripen, and we have to eat, and we are glad. We do not want their good lands; we want our rocks, and the great mountains where our fathers lived. We are very poor; we are very ignorant; but we are very honest. You have horses, and many things. You are very wise; you have a good heart. We will be friends. Nothing more have I to say." *Ka'-pu-rats* is the name by which I am known among the Utes and Shoshones, meaning "arm off." There was much more repetition than I have given, and much emphasis. After this a few presents were given, we shook hands, and the council broke up.

Mr. Hamblin fell into conversation with one of the men, and held him until the others had left, and then learned more of the particulars of the death of the three men. They came upon the Indian village almost starved and exhausted with fatigue. They were supplied with food, and put on their way to the settlements. Shortly after they had left, an Indian from the east of the Colorado arrived at their village, and told them about a number of miners having killed a squaw in drunken brawl, and no doubt these were the men. No person had ever come down the cañon; that was impossible; they were trying to hide their guilt. In this way he worked them into a great rage. They followed, surrounded the men in ambush, and filled them full of arrows.[7]

That night I slept in peace, although these murderers of my men, and their friends, the U-in-ka-rets, were sleeping not five hundred yards away. While we were gone to the cañon, the pack-train and supplies, enough to make an Indian rich beyond his wildest dreams, were all left in their charge, and were all safe; not even a lump of sugar was pilfered by the children.

September 20.—For several days we have been discussing the relative merits of several names for these mountains. The Indians call them U-in-ka-rets, the region of pines, and we adopt the name.

---

[7] The murder of the two Howlands and Dunn was committed at what is now known as Ambush Waterpocket, south of Mount Dellenbaugh. (Ed.— 1915)

The great mountain we call Mount Trumbull, in honor of the Senator.[8] Today the train starts back to the cañon water-pocket, while Captain Bishop and I climb Mount Trumbull. On our way we pass the point that was the last opening to the volcano.

It seems but a few years since the last flood of fire swept the valley. Between two rough, conical hills it poured, and ran down the valley to the foot of a mountain standing almost at the lower end, then parted, and ran on either side of the mountain. This last overflow is very plainly marked; there is soil, with trees and grass, to the very edge of it, on a more ancient bed. The flood was everywhere on its border from ten to twenty feet in height, terminating abruptly, and looking like a wall from below. On cooling, it shattered into fragments, but these are still in place, and you can see the outlines of streams and waves. So little time has elapsed since it ran down, that the elements have not weathered a soil, and there is scarcely any vegetation on it, but here and there a lichen is found. And yet, so long ago was it poured from the depths, that where ashes and cinders have collected in a few places, some huge cedars have grown. Near the crater the frozen waves of black basalt are rent with deep fissures, transverse to the direction of the flow. Then we ride through a cedar forest, up a long ascent, until we come to cliffs of columnar basalt. Here we tie our horses, and prepare for a climb among the columns. Through crevices we work, till at last we are on the mountain, a thousand acres of pine land spread out before us, gently rising to the other edge.

There are two peaks on the mountain. We walked two miles to the foot of the one looking to be the highest, then a long, hard climb to its summit. And here, oh, what a view is before us! A vision of glory! Peaks of lava all around below us. The Vermilion Cliffs to the north, with their splendor of colors; the Pine Valley Mountain to the northwest, clothed in mellow, perspective haze; unnamed mountains to the southwest, towering over cañons, bottomless to my peering gaze, like chasms to the nadir hell; and away beyond, the San Francisco Mountains, lifting their black heads into the heavens.

---

[8] Lyman Trumbull (1813–1896), Senator from Illinois and the co-author of the Thirteenth Amendment to the United States Constitution.

We find our way down the mountain, reaching the trail made by the pack-train just at dusk.

Two days more, and we are at Pipe Spring; one day, and we are at Kanab. Eight miles above the town is a cañon, on either side of which is a group of lakes. By the side of one of these I sit, the crystal waters at my feet, at which I may drink at will.

THE END

Printed in Great Britain
by Amazon